BIAS, RACISM &
the BRAIN

How we got here & what needs to happen

JASON GREER, MSW, MHRIR & PHIL DIXON, MSc.

with JEROME GREER, PhD & TOM RIEGER

OBI
PRESS

OBI Press
Oxford, North Carolina, USA

ISBN-13: 978-1-7338307-6-8

First edition

Copyright © 2020 Phil Dixon, Jason Greer, Jerome Greer

BIAS, RACISM & the BRAIN

JASON GREER, MA. & PHIL DIXON, MSc.

with TOM RIEGER & JEROME GREER

OBI PRESS

Heads up! Warning! Watch out! Do not try this at home!

The neuroscience aspects of this book are based on research and the opinions of the authors. They are intended to provide interesting and helpful information about the brain as it relates to what is going on around us.

To the best of our research abilities, the information is accurate at the time of publication.

The information provided is NOT, however, intended to give medical, health, psychological, psychiatric, therapeutic, or any other professional advice whether related to those fields or otherwise.

The reader should NOT use the information provided as a substitute for the guidance of specialized health care providers.

BIAS, RACISM &
the BRAIN

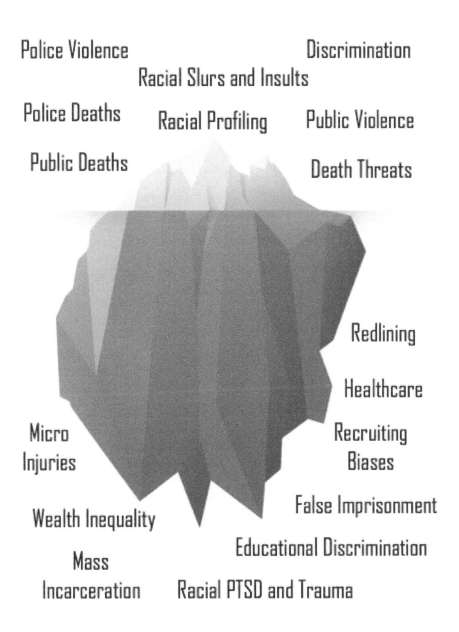

Police Violence

Discrimination

Racial Slurs and Insults

Police Deaths

Racial Profiling

Public Violence

Public Deaths

Death Threats

Redlining

Healthcare

Micro
Injuries

Recruiting
Biases

False Imprisonment

Wealth Inequality

Educational Discrimination

Mass
Incarceration

Racial PTSD and Trauma

Table of Contents

Foreword(s)
Dedication

Appendices

References

Foreword – Jerome Greer

I turned 83 years as of September 8th, 2020. I would like to tell you that my life has been perfect, but I learned a long time ago that there's no point in lying. I have lived long enough to be called a Negro, Afro American, African American and a couple of choice words in between that I choose not to repeat, but through it all I have been a vigilant witness of the best and worst this country has to offer.

The Ku Klux Klan burned a cross directly across from my Daddy's farm when I was five years old. I have seen black men killed for simply looking at white women. I have been cursed at and thrown in jail for leading non-violent protests against segregation during my college years at Tennessee State. But for every ill there is always a blessing. I have long grappled with the notion of racism in America. Why does racism exist and more importantly why do we need to struggle so mightily to eradicate it? This country put a man on the moon, but we haven't figured out how to get along. Never in my lifetime did I think we would ever find an answer to this centuries-old plague until I came across the work Phil and Jason have put together. I am proud to say that Jason is my son.

What you will find in this book is a telling of my story intermingled with my son's life as a black man in America. But more importantly, you will come to understand that there are so many stories playing out in our brains, in such a way that we often can't tell truth from fiction. Love is truth…racism is fiction. At 83 years of age I didn't think it was possible to teach me anything new, but Phil and Jason are on to something big. This is their legacy, just as my son is my legacy.

So, this is my only ask of you…be open and don't forget the things that really matter in life. Be kind to each other, because one day you will understand that money, fame, education and all the things we strive for in life are fleeting. The only thing that really matters is love. So, in other words, let's get past this racism thing so we can get to loving and appreciating each other. Take care!

Dr. Jerome A. Greer,
Peoria, Illinois
September 2020

Foreword – Neil Kiefer

Jason and Phil's book- "Bias, Racism and the Brain"- comes at a time in our world that I believe so many can benefit from taking the time to read. Learning about Jason's real-life experiences, many of which were sadly eye-opening, certainly educates any uninformed, white reader, via real life examples of what blacks have dealt with for way too long. The book also enlightens us on how our emotional and logical brains operate relative to racism.

Their book also provides the reader with many helpful suggestions on how we, as well as our organizations, can directly confront issues of systemic racism, so we can all move forward together in a positive direction. I highly recommend this book for all to read and especially my white colleagues, who will learn much about listening with empathy, putting values into action and to be encouraged to "step on the glass".

Neil Kiefer Esq.,
President & CEO of Hooters, Inc. and affiliated companies,
Clearwater, Florida

Dedication

To all of the people that have suffered or died as a result of racism or racial injustice

And

To all of the people who are working to change racism and racial injustice

Chapter One: Introduction

<u>Jason</u>

In many ways, the idea for this book started in 2010 with the weirdest request I had ever received. My client phoned me in a complete state of panic. He said, "Jason, there's been some racially charged incidents in my New Jersey warehouse. The black and white employees are hurling racist stuff at each other, and it's clear if we don't do something, there's going to be fights all over the warehouse. It's going to be like the LA riots all over again, and I can't have this."

After listening to my client run down the details, I asked him, "What do you need me to do?" He said, "I need to get some diversity training for my managers and the employees before it turns into World War III." I said, "Okay, I don't know much about diversity training, but maybe I can find you someone…" My client didn't even let me finish the statement. He said, "Look, I don't have time to vet a bunch of diversity trainers. I'm not even sure I believe in diversity training. But I believe in you and I know you can create something to help us."

I was flattered and honored that my client believed in me, and if you know anything about being a consultant, it's rare that you ever get any kind of praise. We always get the blame, but we rarely get praised so we try to soak up these moments. But my feeling of pride was cut short by his follow up comment. He said, "Plus, you're the only black guy that I know. People really, really like you, so I'm going to pay you double your rate to fix this for me. I need you in New Jersey by Thursday at the latest." Now mind you, we were having this conversation on a Tuesday evening. I assured him that I'd be there on Thursday armed with the diversity training that was going to be something he had never seen before. The reason why I said it was something he had never seen before was because I had absolutely no idea what I was going to do.

We got off the phone and I was overwhelmed by intrigue and panic. I was intrigued because diversity training was a new endeavor for me. The panic was a direct result of the fact that I had no idea what in the hell I had gotten myself into! Then a familiar feeling hit me deep down in my soul…I was having a WWPD moment. WWPD is short for "What Would Phil Do?" Phil Dixon, my coauthor on this book, is one of my best friends in the world. He also happens to be one of the smartest people I've ever encountered. So, I dialed up Phil's number, made some idle small talk about kids, dogs, that kind of stuff, and then I just blurted out, "Look, bro. My client wants me to conduct diversity training for his warehouse in the next day and a half."

Phil in his distinctive British accent said, "Congratulations, my friend." I said, "Hey, thanks Phil. I appreciate that. But here's the catch. I have no idea what I'm going to talk about. I mean, my client said he wants me do diversity training because I'm the only black guy that he knows. But what the hell am I going to talk about for two hours? How I get my hair cut? What it's like being a black male? What it's like being a pigeon-toed black male? What am I going to do?!" Phil started laughing and said something to the fact that it sounded like my brain was in a threat state. I responded with, "What is a threat state and what does it have to do with my brain? I called you to talk about diversity training, not the brain, Phil."

Phil proceeded to share with me the work that he was doing in the world of neuroscience (also known as brain work!). He went on about "ingroups" and "outgroups", "reward and threat states," and how our society has evolved but our brains are still stuck in the days of our ancestors. Now the "threat state" talk started making sense. From a race perspective, we have been talking about the need to get along somehow, some way, for centuries, yet we can't ever seem to get over the proverbial hump. Phil started to explain to me that our brains are story generators and make up stories about the outside world.

Over the course of our discussion, He and I mapped out what a brain-based diversity training would look like. We realized that the term "diversity" is a trigger word for many people. When they find out that they are required to attend a mandatory diversity training, there are a multitude of thoughts that bombard their brains. Some people may be excited about the possibilities of what they will learn. Whereas others may feel like this is just another vehicle to make white males and white females feel like they are the sole source of everything that is wrong in this world. Phil graciously spent about four hours on the phone with me. We developed this really nice PowerPoint deck and I booked my flight to New Jersey and off I went.

I arrived in New Jersey on a Wednesday evening. I made my way to the hotel and immediately plopped down on my bed. I have to admit that I was scared to death about what this training was going to look like. This was completely uncharted territory for me. Not only was I going to be talking about diversity, but I was also going to be talking about the brain, which was something I didn't quite understand at the time. But I just knew that it made sense because when I thought about my own personal biases, they never made sense. Where did they come from? I had stories in my mind about people that I had never met before. Stereotypes of things and people that I had heard when I was a kid that were still playing out in my adult life.

As I lay on my bed, I started to visualize what this training would mean to my client's employees. Would they get the fact that it's their brains that are standing in the way of their ability to relate to other people? Would I be able to convey it in such a way that I made them feel like it was okay that they held biases - because we all hold biases? I just wanted to be able to educate them on the reality that discovering the root of the stories playing in our minds is the key to overcoming these biases.

Fast forward a few hours to Thursday morning when I was standing in front of a group of 50 or so employees who were all staring at me with those eyes that said, "Man, you better deliver something good because if not, there's going to be trouble." Blessedly, I ended up giving the training of my life. The participants loved the training because I focused their attention on the one thing that we all have in common...our brains. I explained to them that the good thing about our brains is that it's a story generator and it always wants to keep us safe. On the other hand, the bad thing about our brain is that it's a story generator and it always wants to keep us safe.

Our brains are constantly telling us stories about the outside world that may or may not be true. As we made our way through the training, grievances became conversation points. Black employees opened up about their issues with the white employees and the white employees did the same. My client, who's also the owner of the company, looked in and gave me the thumbs up. In hindsight, I don't think he really cared what we were talking about. He was just happy that I had potentially saved him from future EEOC claims. Phil Dixon made me believe that the biggest challenge for race relations in this world is not what we see with our eyes, rather it's what our brains perceive about others.

Since that first experience, I've fine-tuned the "Diversity & Brain: What's Your Story?" training into a powerhouse experience. I've conducted diversity trainings for many Fortune 100 companies, the United States Army, as well as not-for-profit organizations.

Fast forward again, this time ten years to Saturday morning in early June 2020. I phoned Phil as he was driving in his car with his wife, Cathy.

Phil

"Hey Bro. Do you have a quick second? Can I ask you a question?"

That is how Jason has started many great conversations that we have had.

He continued. "What's going on? Why has the George Floyd murder resonated with people so much, whereas all of the other people who have been killed haven't had the same effect? Can you tell me what is going on in people's brains? And would you be willing to write a book about it?"

For me, that's how this book got started. It is, essentially, in three halves. Yes, we meant that! In the first half, we will introduce you to the stories of Jason Greer, and his father, Jerome Greer. We will talk about how the brain works and explore what was happening in the brains of some of the characters involved in the major events in the lives of Jason and Jerome.

In the second half, we will pull it together and suggest some ideas for us all as we move forward, hopefully into a world that is reconciling itself to becoming a far more post-racist way of being.

We finish the book, with a number of Appendices. This is what we call the third half. In the appendices, we have included things that have some extra detail that some readers may enjoy exploring.

En route, you will learn some amazing things about Jason and Jerome Greer - and some amazing things about your brain. Hopefully they will be things that will cause you to pause, reflect and change. Things that will change how you deal with the world on a day-to-day basis. Specifically, things that will cause you to respond more appropriately to the multi-cultural world that we live in.

In writing this book, something strange, or at least different, has happened. I have written three other books and when people have asked me about them, I have told them a little about the topic to which they have politely replied something to the effect of "That's nice" and have changed the subject. In this instance, however, when people have asked me about the topic, I have received three generic types of response, in order of frequency:

The first has been an immediate defensiveness about how they, personally, are not racist. Then they go on to explain why they are not racist, and in doing so often blunder into serious racist territory.

The second is that I shouldn't have taken this subject on as it is too difficult, too contentious and maybe even too dangerous.

The third is that it seems like everyone feels free to give me their opinion about the topic, completely unsolicited, often not very thoughtful, but always subjectively and passionately delivered.

But one thing has become very clear to me while writing this book. I can ask many questions about race and racism. I can have may conversations about race and racism. I can do tons of research. I can attempt to capture it in a book such as this. But, as a white Caucasian male, I can never get to the essence of what it must have been like to grow up as an African American under the Grim Reaper's cloak of Racism.

The Two of Us

We wrote this book because people asked us to. During the Black Lives Matter crisis of May and June 2020, many people started asking questions of Jason; what is going on, why is this happening, what should I be doing about it and how should I now behave? Like Jason, People started asking me, what's going on in our brains? The current swell of interest in Black Lives Matter had followed immediately upon the heels of the COVID-19 crisis. They asked, "Why am I feeling the way I am feeling? Are they connected?"

At the time, there were many opinions out there and many published articles, some of them well-informed and others, not so much. But none of them blended real world aspects from the black experience with a formal, neuroscience approach on what is happening, why it is happening and what we can do about it. That is our purpose and approach with this book. To try something new. To present, as far as we can, a balanced, evidence-based approach.

We have focused this book primarily on Jason's experience growing up as a black person in America. He is a well-educated, highly successful African American male. It goes without saying, that his is not a unique perspective. Unfortunately, his experiences are way too common, for other African Americans, male or female, or other persons of color in America. Many people are subjected to the same, similar or parallel experiences, either directly or indirectly.

So, who's the book intended for? We are tempted to say everyone, but that would be a cop out. ☺ Seriously, if you have been impacted by racism, if you have been racist, or you are trying to do something about the racist issue, then we have written this for you. In the latter category, we see it being used by Human Resources professionals, Learning & Development practitioners and anyone directed to develop DBIE (Diversity, Belonging, Impact and Equality) programs.

As we talked more and more about the issues, we started to realize that there were some impacts that were direct, immediate, and observable. The murder of George Floyd was a pivotal event, but there were many other shootings or deaths as you will see later on in this background section. There were also many occurrences of the use of excessive force by the police. Then there were the deaths and violence caused by members of the public at large. In addition, there was the wide-spread delivery of racial slurs and slights.

These were all issues which were in your face, if you cared to pay attention. But then we started to identify and research the many other impacts which were much more hidden. Systemic discrimination. Red-lining. Educational discrimination. Recruiting biases. Healthcare biases. These impacts were buried much deeper into the various systems of our supposedly civilized society.

That was when we landed on the iceberg metaphor. It is not a new metaphor but expresses what we were hearing about the racial issue. There's a lot more going on, relatively unseen, under the water than what we can more easily observe above the water. And that metaphor tracks exactly with what happens with respect to racism.

There are some obvious things that we see on top of the water, but there is a huge amount of racist activity that goes largely unseen, i.e. under the surface of the water.

And let's be clear about another aspect; the racism iceberg has been around for a long time; it didn't start with George Floyd. It's not even clear exactly when it started, but for African American racism, it started at least several hundred years ago. In the case of racism or discrimination against other particular groups, clearly it is possible to trace it back much further.

And while this topic has been brought into focus by the current attention to Black Lives Matter, the story is the same for many ethnic groups.

Furthermore, it is very clear that racism is just the result of one aspect of bias. The sad thing is that we still, in 2020, see so many other biases being played out, both in the US and the rest of the world, an example of which is the recent announcement that Poland is leaving the treaty on Violence Against Women. [i]

Before moving on, we thought it might be of interest to have a brief discussion about racism itself, including a definition. We are indebted to a recent article by Roberts and Rizzo [1] that provides us with a great starting point. First of all, a definition of racism:

> " … *a system of advantage based on race that is created and maintained by an interplay between psychological factors (i.e., biased thoughts, feelings, and actions) and sociopolitical factors (i.e., biased laws, policies, and institutions)"*

They identify seven factors that contribute to racism in America, as follows:

➢ Categories, which organize people into distinct groups by promoting essentialist and normative reasoning
➢ Factions, which trigger ingroup loyalty and intergroup competition and threat
➢ Segregation, which hardens racist perceptions, preferences, and beliefs through the denial of intergroup contact

---

[i] The Council of Europe Convention on preventing and combating violence against women and domestic violence, better known as the Istanbul Convention, is a human rights treaty of the Council of Europe against violence against women and domestic violence, which was opened for signature on 11 May 2011, in Istanbul, Turkey.

- ➤ Hierarchy, which emboldens people to think, feel, and behave in racist ways
- ➤ Power, which legislates racism on both micro and macro levels
- ➤ Media, which legitimizes overrepresented and idealized representations of white Americans while marginalizing and minimizing people of color
- ➤ Passivism, such that overlooking or denying the existence of racism obscures this reality, encouraging others to do the same and allowing racism to fester and persist

We expand on some of these categories in our section on "Other brain influences." (See page 122)

While their paper is short on what to do moving forward, it is very approachable and readable, and we strongly recommend it. It does provide us with this basic seven-part taxonomy for what we, as a society, need to address as we move forward.

Nature or nurture? Not one of us is born to be racist. It seems that social preference based on race starts to occur between 2.5 and 5 years old [2]; prior to that, although racial differences are discerned, there is no preference based on race. We become more or less inclined to have preferences and make distinctions about race as we age.

With regard to the chapters that focus on the brain, we base many of our models on the models that have been developed in other books that the authors have published. In addition, we quote portions of those books, with permission from the authors and the publisher. If you wish to delve deeper into those models, we have listed those books in our reference list. [3, 4, 5] For those readers who wish to explore our data and sources in more detail, where we think it useful, we have included those references as well. To avoid interrupting the flow of the book, we have added them at the very end. We have also attempted to keep them to a minimum and, in terms of "useful" we have only included them when they are either intriguing or possibly controversial, and we have used a mixture of classic references and new discoveries about the brain.

If what we have written triggers your interest, we have included a bibliography of books, magazines, movies and podcasts in Appendix F.

As authors, together with a group of trusted advisors, we have done our best to pull together a book that might move the issue forward. But we clearly know that there is a lot more knowledge out there that would help even more. If you have suggestions of approaches that you know work, whether at the individual level, the organizational level or the community level, then please contact us at the email below; with the current technology of book production, it is easy to add new ideas in.

Jason.Greer@GreerConsultingInc.com.

Finally, all proceeds from this book will be donated to one or more charities that support the fight against racialism and discrimination. For the first five years, these will be:

Black Women's Health Initiative	www.bwhi.org
Emmett Till Legacy Foundation	www.emmetttilllegacyfoundation.com
Glaad	www.glaad.org
Thurgood Marshall College Fund	www.tmcf.org
Father Support Center	www.fathersupportcenter.org

Chapter Two: How we got here

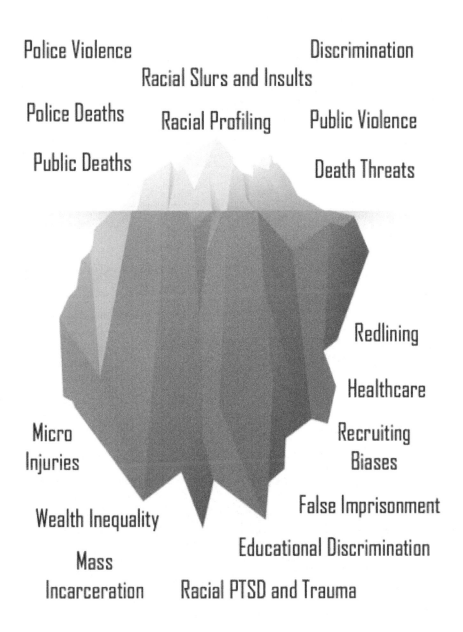

Police Violence

Discrimination

Racial Slurs and Insults

Police Deaths

Racial Profiling

Public Violence

Public Deaths

Death Threats

Redlining

Healthcare

Micro
Injuries

Recruiting
Biases

False Imprisonment

Wealth Inequality

Educational Discrimination

Mass
Incarceration

Racial PTSD and Trauma

Jason & Jerome Greer

Jason Greer is an only child born in St. Louis, Missouri in 1974. He was raised in Bridgeton, Missouri and attended grade school at St. Lawrence the Martyr Catholic School and Lutheran High School North. He was enrolled at Valparaiso University, Indiana from 1992 to 1996, where he was awarded a BSW in Social Work. He then went on to Washington University in St. Louis, to study for a Masters' degree in Social Work. Upon graduation Jason worked for the State of Illinois Department of Children and Family Services as a case worker, following which he worked for the Illinois State Board of Education. He left this role (2000) to pursue a second Masters' degree, this time in Human Resources and Industrial Relations, University of Illinois, at Urbana-Champaign, after which he accepted a position as a Federal Agent with the National Labor Relations Board and was with them for two and a half years. Jason later went on to found Greer Consulting, Inc., an employee relations and diversity management consulting firm. Jason has been cited by the Wall Street Journal, Forbes, and Fox News as one of the top Labor and Employee Relations Consultants in the United States. He now resides in St. Louis, Missouri with his wife Tiffany and their daughter Jada.

Jason's father, Jerome Greer was born in St Louis, Missouri in 1938, the youngest of eight siblings. Jerome's family owned some land in Tennessee, so when he was four years old, they moved to Denmark, Tennessee to become farmers. He started picking cotton when he was four! He says that's where he really learned to work. He attended school at Greer Elementary School and Denmark High School. He enrolled, at the age of sixteen, at Tennessee State University where he was awarded a BSc in Mathematics. He left Tennessee and worked for one year in St. Louis as an administrative assistant in the St. Louis Public School system before returning to Tennessee to study for a Masters' degree in Public Administration at Fisk University, Nashville in 1971. Jerome then went to work as the Principal of Garfield Elementary School in the Normandy School system. During this time, he earned a PhD in Educational Psychology from Nova Southeastern University. His dissertation was on the "Post Psychological Effects of Post Kindergarten Children." Jerome accepted a position as the Principal of Irving Elementary School in Dubuque, Iowa in 1991. He retired in 2004 as the Assistant Superintendent of the Peoria Illinois School system but came out of retirement in 2006 to serve as the Principal of Loyola Academy of St. Louis. He is now officially retired and resides in Peoria, Illinois with his wife, Elaine Greer.

Let's hear from Jason about his and his Dad's story

a) Jason: Looking back - That was then

"We're still white, we're still free and we're still running this country."

Those were the words spoken to Jason minutes after the orator in question, let's call him James McTavish, [b] had been sentenced to imprisonment for hate crimes, amongst which were burning crosses. This was in 1993, not the late 1800's!

Let's rewind two years, and describe what led up to this incident.

Cross Burning

Have you ever heard of the O.C. moment? The O.C. moment can better be described as the "oh crap moment!" This is the moment that the proverbial crap hits the fan. If you're anything like me you probably have an "oh crap" moment every single day of your life, but my first true genuine the "stuff has hit the fan" event happened in 1991. As mentioned above, I was a senior at Lutheran High School North in Saint Louis, Missouri, which was 60% black and 40% white. My father, Dr. Jerome Greer, had been a principal at Garfield Elementary school, part of the Normandy school system, for 20 plus years. My mother, Elaine Greer, had been a nurse at Saint Mary's Health Center in Clayton, Missouri for about 25 years.

My father had a PhD in Educational Psychology, so was well qualified to take on a senior role in any school system. He wanted to be promoted to a central administration role or find a position in another school system, perhaps as a principal in a larger system. My father noticed that many of his white colleagues with similar degrees and experience were being promoted into positions as superintendents, so he decided to apply for some positions throughout the country.

As you will recall, in the late 80's and early 90's the conversations around affirmative action were the big controversial topics of the time. School systems were bringing in applicants of color in order to fulfill quota requirements. They had to interview a certain number of applicants of color. My father was flying all over the country interviewing and, to me, it was so cool. My father is an amazing man, so full of charisma and intelligence, with a true passion for education, so we just knew that he

---

[b] Fictitious name in order to protect the not-so-innocent

was going to get a big-time job. He was interviewing in places like California and Texas, which seemed like big-time for us. Every time he got home, he would say, "Jason, I had a great interview. I think this is the big one, son!"

But over time, my father received rejection letter after rejection letter. We noticed that the rejection letters usually followed the same script, "Dr. Greer, thank you so much for interviewing with us. We love your passion, your energy and your commitment to education. Unfortunately, we cannot offer you a job because we need to see that you have experience working with a different subset of children and academic environments." The Normandy school system is a school system that is largely African American. So, a "subset of children and academic environments" was code for "white kids." All of the school systems that he was interviewing with wanted to see that he actually had experience working with white kids. His experience was with black kids.

But there was one school district that went out of its way to recruit my father. The Dubuque Iowa school district offered my father a principalship over Irving Elementary School. My parents had been married for 30 years at that point, so they decided that they were going to do a commuter marriage for a while because they were not going to take me out of high school for my senior year. We moved my father to Dubuque in the summer of 1991. It was the first time that I had ever been treated like a VIP because we met the Mayor of Dubuque and we got complimentary breakfasts, lunches and dinners. I loved all this attention so much that I tried to convince my parents to let me move to Dubuque. I couldn't figure out why the city was being so generous to my family, but I just figured that they had fallen in love with my father, so they wanted to show their appreciation.

My father and I made the agreement that he would drive to St. Louis every weekend so he could watch me play football. Every Friday after work my father would drive 6 hours to see me and my mom. Within a couple weeks I noticed that there was something different about my father. He seemed to be carrying this...emotional heaviness about him. He would immediately deflect attention away from himself whenever I would ask him what was wrong. What I eventually discovered was that my father was holding a secret from my mom and me.

It turned out that he was targeted by the Ku Klux Klan and that they had burned a cross in protest against my father. Initially it seemed that they took issue with his being announced as the first black principal in the history of Dubuque Iowa. But it was bigger than that. Dubuque had created a program called the Constructive Integration Plan by which they were going to recruit over 100 black families into Dubuque over the course of 10 years. My father and my family became the public faces of this program because we were the first family to come to the city under this program. The problem was that none of us, my father included, had any clue about the Constructive Integration Plan. Things started to make sense after a while. My mother and I were still living in St Louis and were receiving harassing phone calls and notes in the mail, among other things, from what we later discovered, was the KKK. The KKK formed a group called the National Association for the Advancement of White People and the sole intent of their organization was to harass our family and the few black people in Dubuque.

I didn't know what to make of any of this. I was used to being called nigger and spook. In fact, I got called nigger so much that it lost its effect on me. But this? Burning crosses? Death threats? All because my father was a principal in a town that I had never heard of before. All I wanted to do was play football, hang out with my friends and enjoy my senior year in high school.

But life hit me harder than I was prepared for. You see, for my parents this was nothing new to them. My mother was in the first desegregated class at Crystal City High School. She was used to white teachers and students telling her "niggers don't belong in this high school." My mom had experienced more racism by the age of 18 then I will ever experience. My father saw his first burning cross when he was 5 because the KKK burned crosses in the field across from our family farm. But I didn't understand the meaning behind a burning cross beyond its ability to scare the hell out of me. More importantly I didn't understand why they hated us so much. This was my "welcome to the world" experience. In other words, welcome to a world that hates you because you will never be enough!

The Dubuque experience was different for me and my mother than it was for my father. He had the support of the city, the school, the parents and the kids, whereas my mother and I were left on our own with no support system. It was a terrible time in my life. I watched my Mom, who was always so proud of her career, reduced to the point where she could not even get a job as a certified nursing assistant in a nursing home. Me? I was relegated to a life spent in my bedroom, which was in the basement, because I was too scared to go out.

Jerome became a TV celebrity. He was interviewed on Oprah, the Phil Donahue show and a Japanese TV show. We appeared on 20-20 as a family. He was written up in Time magazine in an article on Dubuque, as well as being the subject of a number of articles in national papers. In effect, he became the sacred cow of Dubuque. Jerome has a saying that goes as follows: "For many white people, they can only have one black friend." He became the community of Dubuque's one black friend. Everywhere he went people were excited to see him and previously disrespectful relationships turned to respectful. On the other hand, it seemed like the city said to us "We like this black guy, but we don't want to deal with you two, i.e. me and my Mom."

> Let's, for a moment, take a step back from Jason and Jerome's stories. Have you ever had an equivalent or parallel experience? Most of us will probably say "No". Have you ever been in a situation where you have been constantly, and unfairly, rejected like Jerome? Maybe. What about being scared to go out your front door for fear of your life, like Jason?

And before we move on, how about James McTavish? What happened to him? He served his years and is now a businessman in, guess where? Dubuque.

Why Forgiveness?

At age 35 I decided that I wanted to move on from the anger that I felt toward the KKK for what they did to my family. I had attended a self-empowerment retreat, for 7 days, in White Sulphur Springs, California, with no cellphones or computers. Just me and a group of twenty really awesome people being led through a series of programs designed to help us achieve the ultimate sense of power and personal development possible. One of the concepts of this program was the idea of forgiveness. The program facilitators asked us to write out a list of people that we needed to forgive as well as a list of people that we would like to ask for forgiveness. So, I took out a sheet of paper and a pen because I had so many people that I needed to forgive for everything that they had put me through.

The problem for me was that each time I went to write a name it always came back to three initials…"K.K.K. (Ku Klux Klan)." This seemed ridiculous to me because, clearly,

I didn't need to forgive the Klan…I mean after all I was now this evolved human being who had spent a lot of money for a 7 day self-empowerment retreat!!! I didn't need to forgive the Klan because I had moved on, right? I began to reflect with the retreat facilitators, on the numerous opportunities where I had shared my personal story. I spoke about my family; my work; my…racism. And there it was. Every story that I told always brought me back to the 17-year old kid being smacked in the face by the sheer hatred of people that didn't even know my name. Hell, they didn't even know what my favorite comic book was. Honestly, I hated the Klan, not so much for what they did to my family, but because they took something from me that I would never be able to get back…they took my innocence.

I realized that I had not forgiven the Klan for taking my innocence, but I also realized just how angry I was at my parents. I felt this sense of shame for being angry at the two people who I loved more than life itself. But I couldn't help it and I couldn't bury it any longer. I felt like my parents lied to me. I felt like everything they ever told me was a total fabrication. You see, my parents told me that I would be able to rise above racism as long as I was polite, respectful, kind, and hard working. They told me that they would protect me no matter what, because that's what parents do for their children. So why did they move me to Dubuque? Why did they insist that I attend Valparaiso University instead of a Historically Black College like Morehouse or Hampton? Why did they allow me to be subjected to all of this cruelty? Why did they leave me to fend for myself? Why did they bring me into this world? At this point I was crying my eyes out, which is a rarity for me because I rarely cry. I had all of this bottled up emotion coming out of me in waves. After composing myself, I knew that it was time to let the Klan go. I also knew that it was time to forgive my parents because they had done absolutely nothing wrong. They believed (and believed correctly) that they had done everything in their power to raise their black son to endure anything and everything this world had to throw at him. They armed me with kindness, emotional fortitude, patience and a thirst for success. But most importantly, they loved me, and I loved them back.

I decided that I needed to do something a bit dramatic in order to really forgive the Klan. Writing their name on a sheet of paper, while hanging out in a high-end retreat center in White Sulphur Springs, California was not going to do the trick. After the retreat ended, I returned home to St. Louis. After setting my bags down, I fired up my computer, went online and found the Ku Klux Klan's website. (Google's an amazing thing because you can find anything these days.) I found their website; I found their email address and I found their PO Box. And I wrote them a letter. I simply said to them, "I started out, writing this letter, because I wanted to forgive you for the things that you had done to my family. But I realize that I want to ask your forgiveness, I want to ask your forgiveness for the things that I said about you in the media, for the thoughts I had toward you and the hatred that I felt. And it's my hope that when and if we ever meet, that we can meet as brothers and sisters in love. Sincerely, Jason Greer". Now, I got a response back from them about three days later, and let's just say we're not going to sit down to have a picnic any time soon. But it didn't matter what they said to me, it just mattered that I let go and that I forgave them.

I then sent a letter to the Telegraph Herald, which is the local Dubuque, Iowa newspaper. I let them know how my family was doing. I let them know that I have forgiven the Klan. But I asked the city of Dubuque to forgive me because I never once said "thank you" to the people who would show up at our door every single day once we had officially moved to Dubuque with cookies, pies, and meals. Every single person that knocked on our door had one central message, "Not everybody in Dubuque is like the KKK. And we're thankful that you're here." The Telegraph Herald did a wonderful story on my letter and my family's experience during our time in Dubuque. The special thing to me was the outpouring of love and support that my father's former students (all of whom were adults by this time) had for him in the comments section of the online version of the article. They talked about how nice he was and how much they admired him. Now, don't get me wrong, there were also a number of people who made negative comments about the article and still blamed my family for the negative attention the city received as a result of the Constructive Integration Plan, but that was to be expected.

I often share my forgiveness story at the conclusion of my diversity trainings. It is a tear-jerker of a story because I take the training participants into the world of my hurt and pain as a result of the racist acts committed against my family. But I also leave them with a story of forgiveness, compassion, and empathy. The reaction to the story is something that I will never get used to. For the most part, white people are most often moved to tears by the conclusion of the story. They walk up to me and tell me how much my story meant to them and they often share their own personal stories of seeing racist acts committed against others. On the other hand, black people often have a completely different take. The most frequent question that I'm asked is, "Why in hell did you forgive the KKK for what they did to you? Why did you let them off the hook like that?" But what few people realize is that forgiveness is not about the other person…it's about you. My mind had been consumed by this mental tape that kept playing over and over again. It colored the way I interacted with people and I was in a constant threat state. The reality was that I was still mentally stuck. It was like I was still 17 years old living out the racial abuse over and over again in a never-ending cycle. I was living in a state of fear and I was tired of it. Forgiveness was not easy, but I firmly believe that it allowed me to let go and move forward with my life.

Had I not forgiven them, then what would have happened to me? I truly believe that I would have been emotionally and mentally frozen in place forever. But words and actions have consequences. In 2014 I was conducting a diversity training for one of my clients in a small town in Missouri. I wrapped the training up with the story of my forgiving the Klan. Afterward people were walking up to me to discuss the training, which is honestly my favorite part of training because I get the opportunity to speak to people one on one. I was in the middle of a conversation with one of the training participants when I felt someone tap on my shoulder. I turned around with the intention of telling the person tapping on my shoulder that I would be with them as soon as I possibly could. I saw this middle-aged white man with a sorrowful look on his face. Before I could say anything, he looked at me and said, "I'm sorry for what we did to your family." I immediately replied, "Sir, it's not your fault. You weren't there." He said, "Yes I was. I lived in Dubuque when all of this happened. I was a part of the cross burnings against your father. I left Dubuque because I was ashamed, and I needed to get out of that place. I never thought I would see him or you ever again. I am so sorry for what we…for what I did to you. You didn't deserve it." I was stunned by what I was hearing. I stood there staring at him and I was at a loss of what to say in response. Here I was staring at someone who played a role in hurting my family and he was…apologizing to me. We just stared at each other for what felt like an eternity without saying a single word to each other.

At some point someone put their hand on my shoulder, and I heard, "I enjoyed your training." I spun around to see who was congratulating me and then I immediately looked back with the intention of at least shaking the hand of the man who apologized to me. He was gone. He must have left the auditorium because I could not find him. I never did catch his name and I was surrounded by a sea of middle-aged white people so it wouldn't be much use to ask, "Did anyone see a middle-aged white man around here?" I'm not sure what happened for the rest of the evening. I must have gone on autopilot because I don't remember leaving the auditorium and I can't even tell you what I had for dinner that night. Somehow, I ended up back at my hotel. The man's apology was the source of my delirium. After all of this time, I finally received an apology in the most unexpected place and time. But more importantly, he saw me. I wasn't just a color or a source of hatred for him. This man saw me. He had every right to sneak out the back door and pretend like he'd never hurt me, but he didn't. He took ownership and apologized to me. I will never forget that moment.

> Once again, let's pause. What about that level of forgiveness? Have you ever had to go to that length to forgive a person, group or organization? Can any of us ever know what it feels like to be so despondent that forgiveness is the only way out?

Am I Your Pet?

I started at Valparaiso University in August 1992. My freshman year was terrible. I recall that there were 753 students in my freshman class but only 16 of us were African American. And I happened to be the only black student in my entire dormitory. This was in stark contrast to my experience in high school at Lutheran North where the student population was 60% African American. I made some wonderful friendships in my undergraduate years, but I found that I was stuck in the middle of two extremes. Here I was at predominantly white campus, surrounded by people, most of whom had never been around black people before, and knowing full well that my new home was Dubuque, IA, a city that literally burned crosses in protest of my family. I was stuck and I had no idea what to do. I went from being this happy go lucky, "life is great" kid, to a defensive and scared young man who saw threats everywhere I looked. I didn't know whom to trust and, more importantly, I didn't know if anyone cared to see me beyond my black skin.

I remember walking through campus on the second day of my freshman year. I was trying to figure out where all of my classes were. As I was navigating my way through all of these foreign looking buildings, I felt something on the top of my head. I instinctively flinched and turned around only to see this white man with his hand in my hair. I asked him "What the hell are you doing?!" He said, "That was awesome!! I've never touched black hair before. It's like a sponge." Before I knew what to say he called out to his friends and they all came over with the express purpose of touching my hair. I told them to "F*ck off" but I don't think they heard me, and to be honest I don't think they cared what I said because I was nothing but a plaything…more of a pet…to them. I started to walk away, and they, of course, followed me – in a very intimidating fashion.

By walking faster and faster, and finally running, I reached the Student Union ahead of them, where I thought I might find some help. I went downstairs where I already knew there would be some people that might be like me. I was lucky. There was a group of black people, and even though I didn't know them, and they didn't know me, I sat down. The white guys that had been chasing me, did see me. Or at least they saw the group. But it was clear from the puzzled looks on their faces and the fact that they were continually scanning the room, that they couldn't tell us apart. They eventually gave up and walked away, but they were laughing the whole time.

Although I escaped on that occasion, I will never forget the way they laughed as they chased after me.

The rest of my freshman year was similar to this experience. Meeting people who had never talked to someone black before. Listening to them tell the most racist jokes in the world but acting confused as to why I would be offended. It was typically followed by something like "But you're different, Jason. You're like us…you know you're really white under that black skin!"

> Consider a few more questions. Have you ever been subject to that level of disrespect? Can you imagine how it felt? Have you ever said something not realizing it would be offensive, until later in life when you knew better? Did the preconceptions of your parents influence how you viewed others who were different than you?

Grade School

Merriam Webster defines a best friend as "a person's closest and dearest friend." I have had the pleasure of meeting some wonderful people in my life and I am so proud to say that my wife, Tiffany, is my best friend in the world, but we have only known each other for 24 years. I say "only" because the writing of this book has made me realize that my closest and dearest friend has been racism. Racism has been a part of my life for as long as I can remember. My parents named me Jason but the society I grew up in labeled me "Nigger" long before I was able to verbalize my first word.

Nigger was the word the neighborhood kids used to describe me to their peers. I was 7 years old and it was the first day of 2nd grade at St. Lawrence the Martyr Catholic School. I was brand new to the school and did not know a single teacher or student. I remember walking into the bathroom and there were a couple of older boys talking in front of the mirror. One of the boys looked at me and asked, "When did they start letting niggers in here?" I put my head down, turned around and walked back to the classroom. I sat down at my desk (mind you I still had to use the bathroom but I decided to hold it because I was scared the big kids would beat me up if I went back to the bathroom) and I looked around my classroom at this sea of white students with faces I did not recognize. Did they think I was a nigger too? Were they upset that I was in their classroom? I remember thinking that maybe I should apologize to them if my presence was upsetting to them. Or maybe I will be extra nice to them and they'll think I'm different than the niggers the big boys talked about in the bathroom. I looked around again, hoping that someone…anyone…would make eye contact with the teacher, hoping that in doing so, she would tell me that she will protect me when the older boys came looking to hurt me. I looked out the window, hoping that I would see my mom or my dad's car pull into the parking lot because I was scared and so alone. My mom always seemed to know when something was wrong with me so maybe she decided to take off work early so she could take me home. Within a couple of weeks, I came to appreciate my classmates. So many of them welcomed me into their homes. We had sleep-overs, and we walked the neighborhoods together. I found true, legitimate friends. But I could not understand why I was always relegated to "Group 3," which was the slowest learning level allowed in this Catholic School, by my teachers despite the fact that my scholastic aptitude tests showed me to be advanced in every category other than mathematics.

One of the things that I really enjoyed about the summer was hanging out with my friends, usually with whomever had a video game machine or a VCR (remember those?) although I never understood why I was the only one that was usually asked to leave before someone's parents came home after work or why one of my classmates asked me not to serve as an altar boy at his grandfather's funeral because, "my aunt doesn't like black people."

Time to review this experience. Have you ever felt that degraded? Was there ever a period in your life where you felt left out? How did that feel? What was it like growing up in your grade school

Urine

I went home to Dubuque for spring break. I had come to accept that we were not going to move to another city, so I made the best of my time at home which basically consisted of hanging out with my parents (which was always fun), watching television and weightlifting. The only time that I would leave the house was to go to the gym. I felt safe with my parents, but I was scared to death by Dubuque. I was in a city filled with strangers, and there were a large number of people that didn't want us there. In fact, there was a commonly held belief that we were the reason why Dubuque received all of this negative national attention and they wished that we would "go back where we came from."

On the Thursday before I was scheduled to go back to campus, I was walking to the gym. I had my Walkman headphones on (hey, it was the 90's!) listening to the sweet sounds of Sade. The reason why I listened to Sade was because she calmed me down. It was not uncommon for people to drive past me screaming "nigger" and giving me the "Heil Hitler salute," which I never knew was actually a thing until I moved to Dubuque. Anyway, I was walking to the gym and I saw this car drive past me. It suddenly slowed down and pulled over to the side of the road a few feet ahead of me. I could tell there were four white men in the car. They got out and were yelling all kinds of things at me. I was starting to back up because I didn't know if they were going try to jump me. I didn't know if I was going to have to fight my way out of the situation…all I knew was I was scared, and I just wanted to go home.

I noticed that this man had a bottle of some kind of liquid in his hand. I couldn't tell if it was a bottle of water or what it was because it had a yellowish tint to it. He said to me, "Nigger, I'm going to kick your ass!" At this point he threw the bottle he was holding, and it hit me square in the chest. I looked down and my shirt was covered in this yellow liquid. I only realized that the yellow liquid was urine because it got in my mouth. I was now covered in someone else's urine. You know the crazy thing about this whole situation? My only thought was, "Who in the hell carries around a bottle of urine?" Other than that, I couldn't think. My head was pounding. I was scared, but it was almost like I was out of body because I don't know what happened next. I just remember running away, trying to find my way home knowing full well that I was lost and scared to death.

I eventually made it home. I walked in the house, screaming, cursing and crying. My mom came running down the stairs. She asked me what was wrong, and I told her. She told me to take my clothes off and get in the shower. I went to the bathroom and brushed my teeth...over and over again because I could still taste that man's urine...only to be hit by the creeping thought of "I have no idea if it was his piss or an animal's piss." I was humiliated. I went upstairs after I showered. I spoke to my mom about everything that happened. My mom is very stoic, definitely not one to outwardly show her emotions, but she is an incredible processer. She listened attentively with concern in her eyes. She said to me, "I know you're angry right now..." I didn't even let her finish her statement. I told her that I wanted to go out and kill that man. I wanted to find him...I wanted to hit him. I was so angry...I was so humiliated and embarrassed. I felt like I was a plaything for white people. Like they could just run up to me and touch my hair without my consent or walk past me and touch my skin in order to see if the "paint job rubbed off" as a white person once said to me. They could call me nigger and I just had to take it. They could throw...urine...at me all because I didn't matter.

My mom told me that the most important thing was that I was still alive, and I did the right thing by running home, which, of course, at that age just made me feel like an even bigger coward because I ran away. She also told me to remember that white people had been doing this to black people for centuries. She talked about Emmitt Till being murdered because he allegedly whistled at a white woman. My mom said, "Jason, you got off easy. Urine? Yes, it's disgusting but it didn't kill you. You're still here. They didn't lynch you, did they? Did they burn any crosses? These words they say to you … use it. They think you're a nigger. That's their problem. Be better than them. Be more successful than them. Work harder than them. But don't you let them beat you. Black people have to work twice as hard as white people. You're a black man in America. This is not going to get any easier for you."

 I was angry because this was not exactly the most comforting conversation in the world, but it was exactly what I needed. There was no sugar coating what I experienced, but more importantly my mom understood that she could not coddle me in the moment. I put my head down and my mom looked at me and said, "Jason, you are not going to let this defeat you. I love you. Your father loves you. But we're not going to talk about this anymore do you understand?" I silently nodded my head and to this day we still have not talked about that experience. What I took away from it was that I was always going to be a target. I needed to be stronger; I needed to be smarter; I needed to be better. I was going to have to be exceptional because that was the only way that I would ever stop being a pet to people who thought so little of me.

Imagine what it must have felt like to have that level of humiliation. Or to have had that level of fear. Or be subject to that level of bullying? Think back on a time when you have had a negative experience. How did you respond?

b) Jason: Understanding what's happening now

<u>**Why Black Lives Need To Matter**</u>

Do you remember how old you were when you discovered that you mattered? Were you 2 years old? Maybe 6 years old? Have you ever even thought about it? I grew up around all white kids. It just kind of seemed like they had it all. The teachers loved them. They were in a community of people who looked just like them. Everyone seemed happy, for the most part. Please don't get me wrong, I grew up with a wonderful mother and father who poured love into me. They were constantly telling me I was smart and kind. They always stressed the importance of education and being respectful to other people.

But the love I experienced in our home was far different than what I experienced the moment I walked outside of our door. I was lucky to have some really good friends in my neighborhood, but I was constantly referred to as nigger and any other adjective the racist white kids could use to describe my black skin. I think my teachers liked me but for some reason, as I mentioned earlier, I was always relegated to "Group 3" which was the Catholic School equivalent of special education. My parents did not understand why I was constantly remanded to Group 3. My father approached my third-grade teacher, Sister Marie, about his concerns. She flat out told him, "I don't think Jason can compete intellectually with the other students in the class." She finally admitted, "I don't think black children are as smart as white children."

The kids in my class were very cool to me, but I spent the bulk of my time diffusing stories about black people from the kids in my neighborhood. There was some weird theory that black people's blood was blue. So, the kids would ask me if they could cut me in order to see my blue blood. I developed psoriasis on my scalp because the white kids would put their hands on my hair because it felt like a brillo pad or a sponge. The show "Good Times" was a popular black show back in the '70s. The titular character "JJ" was the star of the show. He was affectionately referred to as "Kid Dynamite." Since my middle name was Jerome, I became known as "JJ," and asked to say "Kid Dynamite" like JJ from Good Times. I kind of relished in this because it meant that people were at least noticing me. Of course, this angered my father because JJ was just another black caricature in a long line of black stereotypes. I actually got angry with my father when he told me to stop allowing people to call me JJ. People were finally talking to me and I didn't want to go back to being invisible. Nevertheless, I followed my father's instructions, but it didn't stop people from calling me JJ. Well, at least they finally saw me.

It wasn't until I was 14 years of age that I realized that I mattered to someone other than my parents. I attended Lutheran North, a private school in Missouri. Sixty percent of the student body was made up of African Americans. For the first (and only time) in my life I actually saw people who looked just like me. They were from similar backgrounds and the majority were from two parent households. Although I was the "white boy" of the group because of how I spoke, the truth of the matter is that I didn't really care. My teachers saw me. My peers saw me. I...mattered. There were no derogatory nicknames beyond the trash we talked on the football field. I was told that being black was a good thing. Girls actually liked me. No one put their hands in my hair; no one asked me if my blood was blue; the teachers told me I was smart, so I was not relegated to Group 3. The guidance counselor, Mrs. Ijei, looked like my mom. My white basketball coaches, Mr. Hip and Mr. Mueller, actually talked to me without saying things like, "One day you will grow up to be a credit to your race." They yelled at me; they celebrated me; they gave me tough love; they never acted like they believed white kids were smarter than black kids and most importantly...they never called me nigger. For those four years I mattered.

This is why I wish people understood the importance behind Black Lives Matter. I was lucky enough to have four years of my life where I actually mattered; where I felt that I was judged by the content of my character and not by my skin color. I felt proud, bold and invincible. I always imagined that this is how my white friends felt everyday they opened their eyes. The difference being that my parents had to pay to send me to a school that prided itself on developing young minds, who happen to be black. In essence there was an entrance fee to enter this world where you were celebrated for being a young black man or woman. On the other hand, my white counterparts were given an unlimited lifetime pass of a privilege. They knew they mattered to the point that it was not even a conscious thought.

I'm in the minority within my own culture. I had four years of it, whereas most black people will never experience even a single second of what it means to matter in this society. Black Lives Matter is not a call to militarize against the police nor is it a conscious movement to establish some level of black supremacy against white people. We are a people that have never mattered beyond our ability to physically build a nation through the shackles of slavery. We only matter when it comes to dribbling a basketball, singing or rapping. We are taught at an early age that we have to hide who we are in order to live and prosper within a society that we were never intended to be a part of. We are the problem that America has not quite figured out what to do with. Our men die in the streets and white people say, "Why should we help? They need to figure out black on black crime first" or something to that effect. Our women are consistently marginalized as "Welfare queens" and "Too strong to be effective in the boardroom." We are a culture characterized by offensive stereotypes and a persona that seems to strike fear in the collective heart of white America. We are the children that no one wants. When we say Black Lives Matter, we are simply saying...correct that, we are pleading for white America to see us as human beings. One day, I would like for my wife Tiffany and our daughter Jada to experience a life where their black skin is seen as an asset and not a liability. I just want them to know what it is like to be seen as two strong, beautiful, successful women who happen to be black.

> Take a deep breath and think for a moment. Have you ever felt like your life didn't matter? How old were you when you realized that your life did matter? What experience made you realize that you mattered or didn't matter?

Why It Hurts When You Say You Don't See Skin Color

A friend of mine used to live next door to a professional football player. He played for the St. Louis Rams. She would always say "I don't see him as a famous football player, I just see him as a nice neighbor." The problem with this was it was a complete and total lie because she would spend all of her time talking about how much money he made, how famous he was and how great it was that her neighbor played for the Rams. The reality is she did see him as a famous football player, but she deluded herself into believing that she saw him as "just a regular neighbor."

I can't tell you the number of times my white friends have looked at me and said "I don't see you as a black man. I just see you as Jason Greer, my friend." I know their intentions are pure and they come from a good place, but there are times I just want to squeeze them and say "I am so tired of you pretending to be colorblind! Yes, I want you to see me as Jason Greer, your friend. That's awesome but it hurts every time you say that you don't see my color because it's like you don't see me."

They don't realize that the sub-text of what they are saying to me, "Being black is something dirty or something I should be ashamed of." And it never fails that they will have this look of pride on their face every time they say, "I don't see color!" But I have come to realize that white people use the "color blind" statement as a way of deflecting from a conversation on race. The color-blind argument allows them to ignore race because it makes them feel uncomfortable. By telling me that you don't see my color what you are really saying is that "I don't want to consider the impact that racism has had on you. Let's sit down and watch some Netflix!"

This approach makes me feel like you are placing a handicapping condition on something that I am so proud of. I am proud to be black and you should see me a black man. I will not ever stop being black. Your privilege allows you to say, "I don't see color" because you don't want to face the fact that because of this skin I have endured cross burnings, racial slurs, urine, the police, Sister Marie, and legal and public discourses on the humanity of black people. You can't see me as a friend and not acknowledge that I am black because this skin I am in is a badge of honor and I wear it proudly.

> Have you ever had the feeling that you are not being really seen for who you are? What do you think people mean when they say that they don't see color?

The Clutch

I've been big for my age ever since I was 10 years old. My parents went out of their way to properly arm me with everything they could think of to protect me as a black male. They told me to be respectful and always be considerate of other people. What they could not have prepared me for was the "clutch." The clutch is the term that I use to describe the actions that white women typically demonstrate when I walk past them. The clutch is the simple act of grabbing the shoulder strap of one's purse when a black male walks by them. White women have been doing this to me ever since I was 10 years old and the truth of the matter is that I'm not even sure that they're aware of what they are doing. I don't know if they think I'm a thief. I mean it's not like I wake up every morning thinking, "Man! Today is the day! I'm going to go out and steal some white woman's purse in full view of everyone in Walmart! This is going to be epic!"

I usually go out of my way to make people feel comfortable in my presence. I wear an easy smile and I usually have something complimentary to say. Whenever I see the clutch I will either look away or say "I hope you have a nice day" in an effort to help them relax around me. I spend so much time going through every mental detail on how not to look like a thief prior to walking into a store, even if I am wearing a business suit. The worst thing in the world is walking through a store's parking lot late at night. People are watching me, security is watching me and all I want to do is hold up a sign that says, "I promise I won't hurt or steal from you. I just want to buy a book."

But there are times that I wonder what is going on inside the minds of the people clutching their purses. Is there some kind of notice that went out that said, "Today is February 13th! It is Jason's birthday! You know what that means...he's 10 years old! Guard your purses!" Have they all had their purses snatched by someone who looks like me? What am I doing in the moment that makes them think "This guy is going to steal my purse? I better hold on to the shoulder strap!" What is it?

> Do you think that (or a similar) reaction is conscious or nonconscious? What other reactions have you observed?

Code Switching – Duality

W.E.B. Du Bois, an American civil rights activist, and variously described as a leader, Pan-Africanist, sociologist, educator, historian, writer, editor, poet, and scholar, wrote about the psychological challenge of "Always looking at one's self through the eyes" of a racist white society and measuring oneself by the means of a nation that looked back in contempt.

I think I've always felt like a problem. I am not saying this from the perspective of getting in trouble or doing anything illegal; rather I have always felt like I exist in a society that has no idea what to do with somebody that looks like me. I am 6'3 and roughly two hundred and seventy pounds. I am used to being one of, if not THE, biggest man in the room. But I also recognize that this is a double-edged sword. Being big AND black can be off putting to people who are not used to dealing with black people. So, I speak in a way that is gentle and kind so as not to offend. I carry the stigma of the "black tax," which means that I have to work twice as hard as my white counterparts. As part of this black tax, I have learned to become proficient at code switching.

Code switching is a great way of saying that I switch between multiple languages within the context to whom I may be speaking. I only speak American English, but I change my cadence and tone based on the ethnicity and the background of the person or people I'm speaking to. For example, if I am speaking to a group of white men/women from the Midwest I understand that I have to speak in a certain way that will put them at ease with me (especially given my physical size in relation to the majority of the people I encounter in business settings) while also demonstrating to them that I really am smart, in order to establish credibility. Contrast this with my being in the company of African Americans. Depending on the setting I will switch into AAVE (African American Vernacular English), and often times I will relax my physical posture and even increase the tone of my voice because I'm not concerned about being perceived as being physically or verbally intimidating.

Code switching is a survival tool, but it is also a means of succeeding for me. I am quite proud of the fact that I have learned how to move in and out of multiple social and professional circles without losing myself, although I have to admit that this is an exhausting process. I'm myself everywhere I go, but I have to augment certain elements of myself while minimizing other elements in an effort to fit in. Code switching is the unfortunate price I have to pay in order to be taken seriously by the majority.

I code switch effortlessly, because I do not have the room to make mistakes. Being as big as I am means that I tend to go out of my way to make other people feel comfortable in my presence. I have to laugh at jokes that were not meant for me. I need to show that I am smart man without appearing too smart because I don't want to offend the sensibilities of the white people around me. I'm constantly on guard and for as confident as I am in my abilities, you would not believe the amount of time I spend dwelling in self-doubt, mentally replaying every interaction, every conversation, every joke, every word that was spoken to make sure that I came across as though I belonged in the C-Suite.

My white colleagues can show up and just be themselves. They can usually find someone who looks like them, talks like them and walks like them. Maybe they attended the same university or grew up in the same town. Perhaps they like fly fishing or have a particular fondness for a similar hobby. They bond quickly with each other and are allowed to make mistakes and say the wrong things. They are allowed to get angry and yell all the while being praised for their "intensity" and "commitment to excellence" whereas I know the moment I raise my voice someone is going to call for security.

As a consultant I'm used to walking into boardrooms where I'm "the only." By this I mean the only black face. It is always funny to me when I've dealt with an executive exclusively on the phone or via email. She or he may have an impression of me that I am exactly like them. But it never fails that they gently slip in a "I didn't know you were black when we talked on the phone" after we finally meet in person. There's this slight hesitation in their face when their perception of me is confronted by their physical reality with me.

I will admit that this code switching, or duality, is mentally and emotionally taxing because I always feel like I am "on" and I do not have the luxury of ever turning it off. By the time I go back to my hotel room I am literally winded and exhausted. It is like I have to hide the real me behind the veneer of what I need to be in order to exist in this white corporate world.

> Have you ever had the feeling that you are always having to be on and are never able to truly be yourself? Can you imagine a situation where you would be forced to do this?

We Do Not All Look Alike

The great civil rights icon and congressional leader, John Lewis, died on July 17th, 2020 at the age of 80. Mr. Lewis survived a brutal beating by police during the historic Equality march in Selma, Alabama, in 1965. He went on to become a true legend of the civil rights movement and a long tenured United States congressman.

Leaders, such as former president Barack Obama, issued public statements of their admiration and deep sorrow over the passing of the civil rights icon. But two Republican United States senators — Marco Rubio, who's Hispanic and Dan Sullivan, who is white — put social media posts with the intention of honoring the death of John

Lewis, but instead used pictures of the deceased United States congressman and civil rights advocate Elijah Cummings who, like John Lewis, was black.

The cringeworthy thing is that both of them shared photos of themselves shaking Elijah Cummings' hand and they had no idea that this was not John Lewis. Twitter immediately shredded Rubio and Sullivan for "confusing their black guys." But you would be shocked at how often this happens to black people and I'm not sure that I will ever really understand it. For example, my wife and I attend a predominantly white church. We love our church, we love worshiping there, and we've been genuinely accepted by the majority of the congregants. Tiffany and I are involved in volunteer leadership capacities, not to mention the fact that she sings with the worship team. I know I'm probably going to sound biased here, but her voice is amazing.

I'm not sure of the total number of black people that attend our church, but I believe it's no more than maybe 10. So, it is beyond crazy to me that so many of the white people routinely get us confused with each other. I'm 6'3, and I weigh 270 pounds. I'm built like a National Football League linebacker. Believe me when I say that I have a very distinctive look. As one of my friends said, "I don't care what anyone is doing in the room. The moment you walk in, everyone takes notice," because I'm just a big presence. But it never fails that our church brothers and sisters get me confused with our worship leader, Lloyd. Lloyd is a dynamic personality with a singing voice that brings to mind some of the great rhythm and blues singers from the late eighties. Lloyd is cool, he's charismatic, he is stylish, and he's just a fun guy to be around but Lloyd is also six inches shorter than me. We look nothing alike other than the fact that we both have very big smiles.

People will actually come up to me after church service and commend me on how beautiful my singing voice is. Initially, when this happened, I was excited because I love to sing. The problem is, I can't sing to save my life. My voice is terrible. But as they are standing there complimenting me on my voice, they would follow it up with, "I am so glad that you are here singing at our church. Your voice is like an angel from on high. Lloyd, we love you."

After my hopes were completely dashed over the fact that nobody was really telling me that my singing voice sounds good, I would just nod my head and allow them to go on about their day, because they wouldn't believe me even if I told them I wasn't

Lloyd. But it gets really old. There's another African American gentleman at the church who happens to be in senior leadership. This man is incredibly cool beyond belief. He's highly intelligent and very well respected by the church body and the St. Louis community at large and does a great deal of work with the St. Louis police department.

But again, there are people who think that we are the same person, even to the point of arguing with me, to my face, that we look alike. Although we are close in height, the only two distinguishing features that we share are the fact that we both sport low haircuts and we wear glasses. That's it! Our physical features don't look alike, our skin tone is different, our sense of style is different. We are two different people, but they continue to get us confused with each other.

This is so frustrating, especially considering that I attend a church where the bulk of the congregation believe "all lives matter," and yet they can't tell the difference between the few black people at the church.

But this "all black people look alike" phenomenon is not isolated to my church. This has happened my entire life. I've noticed that the people who do this have little to no experience with people of color. It's like they don't have a mental model to tell the difference between people of color.

> What about you? How easy do you find it to differentiate between people who are not of your own race?

What Happens When You're Stuck Between an Outgroup and Ingroup

With all this talk of the brain and how we perceive people from different walks of life, it suddenly dawned on me that it seems like there's no neuroscientific category for someone who walks in between multiple worlds. Let me give you an example. I'm a proud black man. I was raised by two loving black parents. My wife is black, I have very strong pro-black leanings in terms of a belief in equality, the strength of the black family and the fact that I'm a strong supporter of the Black Lives Matter movement. Yet, despite this, I find that I exist on this consistent plane of being in the "black world", but not being of said black world.

I grew up in an entirely white environment. I'm constantly amazed by the number of social media friend requests I receive on platforms such as Facebook from people that I grew up with, all of whom are white. If I'm being honest, I have no recollection of a number of these people. They can recall stories of times from our youth. They can talk about places, dates, but my memory of them is blank.

It used to really bother me because I have a great memory. I can recall the exact issue of the Incredible Hulk comic book that my father used to teach me how to read. (It was Incredible Hulk 194 for anybody who might want to know. Hey, don't hate me, I'm a geek.) But I can't tell you about the people I grew up with outside of my primary friend group. Why do they remember me, but I don't remember them? I used to rack my brain trying to figure out what made me stand out to them. I don't remember being popular. I wasn't known for telling jokes. I was a good athlete, but I didn't really stand out from my teammates before high school. I didn't run like Carl Lewis and I definitely didn't jump like Michael Jordan. I was so unpopular with the girls, that I was eternally banished to the friend zone long before there was a friend zone. In short, there was nothing exceptional about me. So why do I stand in the memories of people who claim to have known me?

The only answer I could come up with was the fact that I was the only black kid. If you look back at all the pictures and things like that from grade school, the class pictures, you'll see a sea of white faces and then you'll see me with my Afro. I was a chubby kid with kind of crooked teeth who was trying to figure out how to fit in while also feeling like life would be perfect if I actually did fit in. That's sort of been my walk in this life, in that, as I've grown in maturity, have grown in experience, met wonderful people, seen amazing things, wonderful education, great career life, I found that I now exist in this world where I am too black for white people, but I'm too white for black people.

I'm always in the state of purgatory (there's my Catholic upbringing coming into play), because I don't always know where I fit. In my professional life, speaking "proper" earns me a certain entrance to corporate boardrooms. I talk as though I belong there. I can relate to people in terms of activities, hobbies, experiences. Now mind you, the majority of the people that I interact with on a daily basis in my professional life are white. I'm in their world, but again, I'm not part of their world. I have to know more about their world than they have to know about mine.

Now flip the script. The people that I interact with in my personal life are so diverse. My group is a mixture of black, white, Hispanic, LGBTQ and Asian. I find that again, there is so much that we can relate to in terms of our experiences, in terms of our perspectives, but I still don't feel like I fully belong. I guess because I've spent so much time as an "other" that I don't know what it means to actually be firmly planted in one world. So now I'm left with the following question: "Where in my life, do I feel a sense of the reward state that we talk about?"

When I'm with my wife, I feel like I'm in the reward state. When I'm with my daughter, I feel like I'm in a reward state. When I'm with my parents, I feel like I can relax and just be myself. But outside of this, even when I'm with close friends, I am constantly on edge because I don't know what it's like to fully be me with other people.

There was a gentleman a long time ago who told me that I was like a chameleon, meaning that I could become whomever and whatever I needed to be based on the situation I found myself in. While this has been an incredible boon for my career in terms of having that skillset, he's actually right because existing on the outside means that I spend a large amount of time observing other people, their habits, their norms, facial expressions, body language; I'm constantly on edge looking for a perceived threat while also trying to make sure that I'm not seen as a threat to whomever it is I happen to be around. This is exhausting, but it's the life that I lead; I don't know any other way to be.

My experiences as a kid in an environment full of people who didn't look like me taught me that I constantly had to scour the environment for threats while also minimizing the perception of my being threatening to them. If I misread the body language of the kids that I was around or the people that I was around, that might mean that I'm the one that ends up getting my ass beat while everybody stands around watching. In college, if I misread the voice inflection or the facial expressions of a professor, that might mean that I was deemed as being one of those "slow black kids" that I heard people talk about; the implication was that I was accepted into Valparaiso University based on affirmative action as opposed to actually earning my way into the university.

If I don't dig deep enough into the verbiage that comes out of a client's mouth, I might give them pause and make them believe they should have gone with the white consultant as opposed to going with me. If I'm walking into my local Walmart and I see a white man who's walking toward me and his body language stiffens up, either that means he's going to attack me, accuse me of something, or I've done something to make him feel as though I'm a threat. So, I spend a great deal of time monitoring my own body language. What am I giving off? What word choice am I using to diminish the presence of a threat? Am I smiling enough? Do I look friendly as opposed to looking menacing?

Part of the struggle of existing in the space between multiple worlds is that I become the "invisible man," meaning they don't have to see me, but I have to see them. And when they do see me, I have to make sure that anything and everything I'm giving off is in accordance with the standards of their community. So, I get back to my original question. What happens when you're stuck between an outgroup and an ingroup? In one group, the color of my skin gets me into the door, in another group, the color of my skin keeps me standing on the outside of that door.

In one group, the color of my skin gets me inside the door, but the moment I open my mouth and I sound like the other group, I'm immediately shown the door because I don't belong. In the other group, they see the color of my skin and they won't ask me in. They hear the sound of my voice and they say, "He's like us," and they bring me in. But the moment that we disagree on a racial topic such as Black Lives Matter versus All Lives Matter, the moment that I reject the notion that Candace Owens speaks for all black people, I'm told that I'm really no different than other black people and they ask me to leave. So, what happens when you're stuck between an outgroup and an ingroup and you can't really be yourself in either group?

> Have you ever had the experience of not fitting in? What must it feel like to not fit in anywhere except within your own close family?

I'm Tired of Not Feeling Safe With You

Okay, I have to admit something. I'm tired of being my white friends' only black friend. Being their only black friend means that I'm constantly in a position of having to explain the black perspective, without any of them realizing that, although I have an opinion on certain matters, I do not speak for all black people. In fact, I remember telling a friend of mine, who just kept inundating me with question, after question, that I am not the "king of black people."

It never fails, that when something race related happens and it makes some major news sources, then I'm inundated with calls, texts, emails and social media posts, asking "Why did this happen?" And if there is an event that involves protests or riots, then I have to hear my white friends say things like, "All those 'thugs' do is burn down their own communities," which, of course, doesn't make any sense to me because how many of the people out on the streets, protesting for racial equality, own a Target or a Walmart?

One more thing that I find difficult to tolerate is when my friends and associates who never, and let me say this again, NEVER talk about Martin Luther King Jr., and likely wouldn't know a single book written by or about him, can't wait to cherry pick MLK quotes to show how we should "love" instead of protest, because love always wins. Uh…for the record, Martin Luther, THE King, was assassinated. In the year prior to his death, he unequivocally stated "a riot is the language of the unheard," but it's quite likely that you missed that because most people believe the only important thing that Martin Luther King ever said was, "I have a dream." Sometimes I just want to scream, "Will you please go out and get some more black friends, so you can make being your friend easier for me? Please?"

You may be asking where does all this frustration come from? Well, it comes from the fact that I've learned the hard way that, although some of my friends like me, it doesn't mean they actually like people who look like me. I'm that racial cover they use when they consciously or unconsciously say something racist, but then they quickly cover it up with, "My best friend is black." They are also the ones who will vote and publicly support politicians who espouse racist rhetoric but will tell me how much they hate racism. My response to this is, "You willingly voted for (*insert name here*), even though the bulk of his or her political base is comprised of white supremacists and racists. You may claim you hate racism, but clearly it is not a deal breaker for you." I listen to my white friends blame the media for inciting conflict and division, as though racism wouldn't exist if it wasn't ever talked about, but I don't remember history books saying anything about CNN, MSNBC, or Fox News causing lynchings, denial of equal rights, and the sheer discrimination and terrorizing of people of color in this country.

In fact, I find that the people who rarely, if ever, interact with people of color, are the ones who believe racism is only "a thing" because of the media. They live in their isolated communities, full of people who look just like them and they guess about the conditions affecting people who don't look like them. They believe racism is a contrivance of the media because they don't know or see anyone who's personally affected by it. It's hard to empathize or sympathize with people you don't know. I know they mean well, when they say, "Jason, I don't see color. I love all of God's people." Well, with all due respect, you are a terrible liar because if you didn't see color, then chances are pretty good that you would have a couple more friends of color besides me. All I want is to feel safe with my friends, I really do, but I'm struggling.

I cannot tell you the number of times I've been out, with my white friends, generally having a good time and then something racist happens, but I'm the only one that sees it. For example, my white friends and I were out for dinner. When it was time to settle up the bill, we all decided that we would pay for our individual meals. I watched my white friends give the waiter their credit cards, but for some reason, I'm the only one he asked for "proper identification" when I handed him my credit card. When I pointed this out to my friends, I was met with, "Maybe he forgot to ask us for our IDs," or, "I'm sure you think it's racism, but maybe you didn't see what you actually thought you saw." What? Does that make any sense? Even when I try to push the issue with my friends, you can usually see the look on their faces that says, "Why do black people always make things about race?"

So, I, like many other people of color, learn to bottle it up because we don't want to be seen as playing the "race card," but let's be honest, who has the real race card? People of color who routinely face discrimination or white people who are generally given the benefit of doubt, based on the color of their skin? I even had a situation with a friend, who happens to be white, where we were having dinner. I excused myself, so that I could use the bathroom. Upon returning from the bathroom, I happened to notice two white men staring at me as I was walking back to our table. I met their respective gazes and I saw one was wearing a shirt with the Confederate flag emblazoned on the front and his friend had a hat with the Confederate flag on the front and the sides. My mind went into overdrive. "Okay, there are two white men staring at me and they're wearing

Confederate flags, so it's a good chance they may not think highly of someone who looks like me. Do I say something, or do I casually walk back to my seat?"

I opted for casually walking back to my seat, although, I was very aware of everyone in the restaurant. I was looking for the exits in the event that these Confederate flag bearers decide they want to single me out, which wasn't hard considering I was the only black person in the restaurant. I looked at my friend and said, "Hey, man, you see those two guys over there? They're wearing Confederate flags and they were staring at me." My friend looked at me and proceeded to remind me of the wise words of our pastor, who is white, that we must respect people, even those we disagree with, and then he moved onto the next topic. I was astounded. I was looking at my friend and thinking, "Wait a minute. I just told you that two white men with Confederate flags were staring me down and you just hit me with a (insert curse word here) quote from our pastor?!" For black people, when we see the Confederate flag, we're automatically reminded of slavery. We're reminded of the fact that the KKK and other racist organizations have historically used that flag as a sign of white supremacy.

Okay, let me break this down to you a little bit deeper. What my father taught me is if you see a truck coming at you and it has a Confederate flag anywhere on the truck, you run and you hide, because they're coming for you. So, I sat there, worried, concerned and ready to leave. I still engaged in idle chit chat with my friend, but I was now totally aware that I was 100% on my own, because if something did happen, I had no faith my friend would have my back. I'm sure he would likely say something to me like, "Well, why didn't you tell me you felt uncomfortable there? We would have left."

This is a valid point, but I'm tired of having to be the one who points out racism to my rather clueless friends, while also having to deal with the very racism that I'm pointing out. What this means is that I have to intellectually quantify racism; then I have to verbalize it to my friends which is followed by the automatic debate of "are you sure it's racism?" all the while, dealing with the emotional toll that comes with being a victim of racism. It is exhausting. It is draining and heart-wrenching and exactly why I'm tired of not feeling safe with my friends. My hope is that, some time, people will go out and start to educate themselves on the lives of people who are not like them.

> How do you think it feels to be always on the lookout for threat and not feel safe, even with friends?

Donald Gardiner [c]

I'm a former federal agent with the National Labor Relations Board. I loved my time with the Board, and it influenced many things in my current business world of consulting. My supervisor was an awesome man by the name of Donald Gardiner. Don was an old school supervisor and an old school federal agent. He gave me a lot of opportunities to learn everything from Labor Board procedures, to serving as a Hearing Officer. It was fun working for him because he always had some bit of wisdom to impart to me and he had this way of treating even the most serious circumstances as though there was a solution.

I was taught by my parents to always refer to people older than me as sir, so naturally I referred to Don as "sir," whenever we spoke.

One day, I was preparing for a hearing, which meant that it was my responsibility to mediate issues between a labor union and the company they were seeking to organize. The attorneys who were representing the company and the union were in the hearing room, preparing themselves for the upcoming process. I was sitting in the hearing officer's chair, which was cool to me at the time, because I was sitting in front of everyone while trying to pretend like I knew what I was doing. Don walked into the hearing room and asked me to step outside, because he had a question about another case. I looked up from reading my hearing officer's manual, and I said, "I'll be right there, sir."

I saw Don turn red as he looked around the room. I noticed the older attorneys looking at him and then looking at me, but I was clueless as to what was happening. I met him outside and Don, in his infinite patience, said to me, "Jason, I really like you. You're a great guy with a good future at the Board, but you're going to have to stop calling me 'sir'." I was stunned because I thought I had done something wrong. I said, "Don, I was never trying to be disrespectful to you. Did I say something to offend you?" Don read my confusion and my hurt, and he said, "Jason, did you notice the reaction of the attorneys of the room when you called me, 'sir'?" I told him that I noticed they kept looking at the both of us, but I figured they were just curious as to why he had asked me to leave the hearing room.

---

[c] Permission given by Don to use his real name.

Don said, "They were looking at the both of us because you referred to me as sir. Those attorneys are older white men like me and we all remember a time when black people were taught to call us sir, because it was about power, not respect." I responded with, "But my father told me to call people older than me 'sir' and 'ma'am,' as a sign of respect. That's all I meant it to be, sir…I mean, Don."

Don put his hand on my shoulder and said, "I get it, Jason, but I don't want anyone believing that I'm treating you like you're subservient to me, just because I'm your supervisor. You may work for me, but I see you as a person, and I hope that you see me as a person. So, from here on out, I need you to call me 'Don,' not sir. This is a different time and it's a different age. You're young, but I'm still a throwback to a time where things were 'separate but equal,' - it might've been separate, but it was very unequal. Now get back into that hearing and go do a great job, Jason."

> What other verbal habits, like Jason's of calling older men, Sir, have you observed? What has been their impact?

The Police

Seven years ago, in 2013, my neighbors gave me the keys to their home and asked me to look after their dog because they were vacationing at the Lake of the Ozarks for five days. The task was relatively simple. All I had to do was go over to their house, take the dog out for his daily trip to the bathroom, fill up his food bowl and make sure that he had enough water to last him for the day. One day, I pulled into their driveway and I reached into my pocket to pull out the housekey. I couldn't find it in my pocket, so I looked in the shoulder rest and finally the glove compartment, to no avail. I happened to notice a man standing on the porch in the neighboring house. I politely waved as I continued looking for the key.

I decided to head home after realizing that I left the key on my kitchen table. Ten minutes later I once again pulled into the driveway and I saw the man from the porch looking around the house where I was dog sitting. He was checking the windows, which was weird to me. I also noticed several people standing in their respective lawns staring at me. He saw me pull into the driveway and walked up to the passenger side window. He asked me what I was doing there. I told him that I was checking on my neighbor's dog and that I had keys to their house. Before I could ask why he was checking their windows he said to me, "I just want you to know that I called the police because you look like you were trying to break into their house." I was stunned! I asked him, "How in the hell can I break into a house that I have a key for?" Apparently, the man had gone to his neighbors and asked them to keep watch while he investigated the house.

I got out of the car to confront the man. I was angry but also highly embarrassed because I felt like all of my neighbors (all white) were judging me for something that I did not do. I wanted to leave but I was scared that would make things worse.

Imagine the scene. There I am standing on a sidewalk. I have this white man accusing me of breaking into a house. Behind me stand white neighbors all holding their cell phones as if they are waiting for the right moment to call the police, who were apparently already on their way, if I give them the slightest indication that I am going to hurt someone. I thought to myself, "What's next? A bottle of urine?" Ten minutes later a police car pulled up. I'm thinking "I'm in trouble…a cop is here." Two minutes later three additional police officers arrived on the scene. That made a total of four police officers. They all stepped out of their vehicles. All four had a hand on their guns. They were staring at me. I was scared…I was humiliated…I was embarrassed…I was a target.

Now let me contextualize this for you. I'm a huge comic book fan. I LOVE the X-Men. I'm what is affectionately known as a "blerd" (black nerd). I'm wearing an X-Men t-shirt that reads, "Magneto was Right," Nike shorts and flip flops. I don't have a gun or any weapon on me. The only thing in my pocket is a wallet. I'm standing there, face to face with the police while looking like the world's biggest blerd. My God…I can't go out like this. My heart is racing. I can't think.

As the officer asked me what my name was, I immediately switched into default mode. I said "My name is Jason Greer. I'm a small business owner. I live in this neighborhood. I have three degrees; I've never done anything wrong and I am not a criminal. I have keys to this house because my neighbors asked me to check on their dog. I've never stolen anything in my life. I mean you no harm. I would never hurt the people in this neighborhood. Please just let me go. I haven't done anything wrong." It's crazy what you think about when you feel like someone is going to kill you. I remember looking at the cops and it struck me that they still had their hands on their guns. I took a look at my neighbors. I wanted someone…anyone…to step in and help me. But I guess that was asking too much. Once again, I was the "only." This time it wasn't the classroom or the boardroom. This time I was standing in the middle of the street surrounded by white police officers and white neighbors, all assuming that I was a criminal.

The police officer asked me for my license or some proof of identity. I told him, "My wallet is in my pocket. I am going to grab my wallet, sir. I do not have a weapon in my pocket." I slowly reached my hand into my pocket to retrieve my wallet. I took the license out and I held it out in front of me. The police officer walked up to me, still with his hand on his gun, took my license and walked back to his car. I guess he checked my license with his computer. I don't know. I just know that I'm standing in the street, pouring sweat, while trying not to make eye contact with the police officers who were locked and loaded. Finally, the officer who took my license walked up to me and said, "Sir, you're free to go. This is clearly a mistake have a good day."

All the officers got into their cars, turned around and left. I looked back at the neighbors who at this point had gathered together in a semi-circle as they watched the events unfold. They dispersed as soon as I turned around and looked at them. As for the neighbor who called the police…he didn't bother to offer an apology or anything of that nature. He just walked inside of his house. I stood there in the middle of the street for what seemed like an eternity. I couldn't move. I was angry; I was embarrassed; I was humiliated; I was scared, and it felt like I was back in Dubuque, I was standing there drenched in piss. I was 18 all over again. I was alone and I didn't matter…no one even had the common decency to ask me if I was okay.

There was this assumption that I was a black man in a neighborhood in which I didn't belong. I didn't have a bomb on me, I've only shot a gun twice in my life at a shooting range. I was no threat, at least in my mind, but I was enough of something to warrant the white man calling the police on me. I was enough of something to warrant the need for four police officers.

This is why I contend that George Floyd could have been me. I watched the video of George Floyd being murdered by former Police Officer Darren Chauvin. Chauvin placed his knee on Floyd's neck for eight minutes and forty-six seconds. Eight minutes and forty-six seconds. He killed that man. I did not have the pleasure of meeting George Floyd. I don't know his family or his friends. I would not recognize his children and prior to May 25th I may have walked past Mr. Floyd and not thought anything about it beyond giving him what our community likes to call the "universal what's up," which is a quick head nod as if to say, "I see you." But as Floyd laid there, screaming for his momma and uttering the words "I can't breathe" I realized that this could have been me on the day the police pulled up because someone suspected that I was burglarizing my neighbor's home.

I've had a number of people ask, "Why didn't the bystanders who were recording the murder of George Floyd step in and save his life?" If you watch the video, you will notice a number of people on the sidewalk, begging former Police Officer Chauvin to take his knee off George Floyd's throat. As the video went viral, I noticed a number of conversations happening on social media platforms like twitter and Facebook asking the question, "Why didn't someone step in to help?" This was usually followed with "Those people watching are just as guilty as those police officers. I would have saved him if I had been there." In fact, many of my friends have echoed the same sentiments. What my friends and the online community have in common is that they are all white. Their privilege allows them to believe that the police officers would have listened to them without any fear of physical harm.

The people recording and watching the murder of George Floyd were all people of color, with the exception of one white woman. I guarantee that if you were to ask them why they didn't help, every single person would have said something to the effect of, "They would have done the same thing to me that they did to George Floyd." Herein lies the emotional duality of being black in America. They saw George Floyd being choked out by Chauvin's knee. They begged and pleaded with that man to let him go and yet they were unable to do anything to help George. Their lack of privilege is what stopped his life from being saved.

White people say, "The people standing there watching should have helped." Black people say, "My heart goes out to the people who had to watch this knowing they were powerless to stop it."

If white people have this much power to tell police officers what they should or shouldn't do, then why didn't my neighbors help me? It could have been me in the street, with an officer's knee on my neck as I screamed out for my mother while my neighbors stood there watching. It could have been me screaming "I can't breathe" shortly before my life passed on. I am George Floyd because I can empathize with his fear and the loneliness he felt in the last moments of his life. I am George Floyd, a large black man whose only crime was being born into a society that never really wanted me. I am George Floyd…WE are George Floyd.

> How about feeling that level of helplessness? Unable to control any aspect of the situation? What about that level of embarrassment?

COVID, George Floyd and Empathy

On Saturday, March 14th, 2020, my wife and I flew into Los Angeles airport, also known as LAX, with only 17 people on our flight. We had planned to stay with friends for a few days. However, on Sunday, March 15th, California Governor Gavin Newsome announced the closing of restaurants and other establishments due to the coronavirus' ability to spread through crowds of people. It became crystal clear that we needed to cut our trip short.

On March 16th, as soon as we landed in St. Louis, we went to Costco and found it packed with customers. We saw people with carts full of toilet paper, paper towels, they had food supplies they knew good and well that they were never going to eat, but it didn't matter. Shelves were almost empty, and people were running around like their hair was on fire. That's just how frantic it was. It was almost like we were living in a terrible horror movie minus the zombies.

Later, we sat on our couch, turned on the television, and tried to digest every piece of news that was being fed to us across multiple platforms. The problem was no one quite knew what coronavirus was, nor how it was being transmitted. There were reports hospitals were filled to the brink with people who were reporting coronavirus like symptoms. It was heartbreaking to hear reports about the hospitals filled to capacity with COVID patients, people dying, loved ones being separated out of fear of COVID exposure, businesses closing down and people losing their jobs. There were reports of people dying and rumors of the virus being transported here from China, in addition to the theory that the virus was being generated by 5G cellular towers. It was complete and total chaos in every sense of the word.

Like so many others we felt like the power was being taken out of our hands by federal, state, and city officials who imposed orders, often conflicting in nature, on Americans without giving us the ability to weigh in on what any of this meant to our collective standard of living. Hindsight being 20/20, it was pretty apparent that our political leaders had no idea what they were doing. The desire was to protect and save as many lives as they could, but it wasn't clear that anyone knew how to do that.

Ultimately all this came down to the fact that COVID was this massive invisible force that brought the world to its very knees. It wasn't just America that was being crippled by this virus, countries all over the world were shutting down long before we did. There was so much uncertainty, and there was this overall feeling of powerlessness.

So, why am I telling you this, when, on the surface at least, it has little to do with racism and discrimination? I am doing so, in order to give you the background and context to what happened next.

The month of March came and went, same with April. Then on May 25th, we bore witness to one of the most heinous acts ever to be caught on video. Police officer Derek Chauvin placed his knee on George Floyd's neck for eight minutes and 46 seconds. Officer Chauvin murdered George Floyd in full view of the entire world.

People around the world, watched a police officer… supposedly a man of justice… commit murder and were suddenly made to question the belief that justice in America was metered out equitably to all people, regardless of skin color.

Now, the platitudes that many white people trumpet out to black people, or people of color in general, when dealing with the police is:

1. Be respectful
2. Don't try to resist arrest
3. Speak to the police officer kindly
4. Be humble in your approach
5. Be gracious because police officers have so much to deal with
6. Remember…police officers are your friends

Based on the vantage point of multiple security cameras, as well as cell phone footage taken by a brave young woman holding her camera on the arresting police officer, it was clear that George Floyd followed all of these advisory rules. He was at least five to six inches taller and much larger than the arresting police officers, yet he never attempted to fight with them. But that did not stop Chauvin from placing his knee on George Floyd's neck for eight minutes and 46 seconds.

Chauvin heard Floyd say, "I can't breathe" multiple times. He screamed, "Mama!" as though he could see his deceased mother in front of his eyes. Did George know that he was going to die? Did his mother come to take him home? All of a sudden everything that white America had been told about police brutality against people of color was in full view.

Now I'm not going to get into the protests that followed, because this topic is being dissected in multiple books, television programs, and social media forums around the world. What really interests me is the question, "*Why did white people respond to the killing of George Floyd when many very acts of brutality had been caught on film in years past?*" Tamir Rice didn't move the needle. Michael Brown barely registered beyond the black community. The same with Eric Garner. And Breona Taylor. What was it about George Floyd? A man that few, if any, knew of beyond his beloved Houston neighborhood? Numerous theories have pointed out that we all happened to be home without the distraction of work, social commitments, kids sporting events, etc. so people had the time to watch as Floyd was murdered in real time. This sounds like a neatly wrapped explanation as to why this impacted white America in a way that it had never before, but it is too simplistic. That may all be true, but I believe there's also another layer which has not yet been fully explored.

During the quarantine and stay at home order, white people were made to feel like minorities by the very institution that was created for them, the government. The average white person had no say; no rights; and no power, just like minorities. Being forced to stay at home made white people feel the same powerlessness that ethnic minorities deal with on a constant basis. Whether we like it or not, COVID created an empathic bond between outgroups in a way that no one could ever have imagined.

But herein lies the challenge for race relations. It took a global pandemic and the subsequent economic turmoil for white people to open their eyes to the sufferings of communities of color, and even this seemed to be a temporary understanding as life returns to normal for people who do not encounter racism in their everyday life.

The fact of the matter is that without empathy, there can be no progress. Without empathy everything just seems like window dressing because it does not dig into the core of what racism truly is, a societal disease that we are all affected by. Some of us just happen to be asymptomatic.

> Why has George Floyd's death resonated with so many people, not just in America, but around the world? Because we had nothing better to do? Or, as Jason has suggested, a wider set of groups felt the same level of helplessness as people of color on a regular basis? Your thoughts?

Jada and George Floyd

On Sunday, June 7th, 2020, my wife, Tiffany and I sat down in front of my computer with our 14-year-old daughter. In a normal world, we see Jada every other weekend due to the custody arrangement we have with my ex-wife, but these are uncertain times. St. Louis County had imposed a COVID-related stay-at-home order, which meant that this was the first time we had seen Jada since mid-March. So much had occurred in the world since we had last seen our daughter, not the least of which was the murder of George Floyd and the protest which followed.

Families from every walk of life were having kitchen table conversations about racism, systemic racism, Black Lives Matter and police brutality with their kids, so we assumed, and you know what they say about people who assume, that Jada had been exposed to some level of dialogue about the events happening around her.

Her white classmates had shamed her for not knowing more about the protest happening in downtown St. Louis and for not being more involved in the BLM movement. Suffice it to say, by the time we picked her up on June 5th, Jada was full of questions and overall curiosity about the George Floyd video, as she put it, "The video my friends can't stop talking about."

At dinner that evening, we caught up on everything that was going on in our lives as we normally do, but then the conversation took a sharp turn. Jada wanted to understand why George Floyd was murdered. She said, "I thought the police were good people. Why would they kill George Floyd? I haven't seen the video yet, but that's all I keep hearing." We assured her there are a number of kind and professional police officers who truly want to do right by everyone they encounter. But unfortunately, there are officers like Derek Chauvin who believed they are above the law and have no regard for the lives of people, especially Black people.

Tiffany then looked at me and gave me what I affectionately refer to as the "Tiffany nod," which translates into "it's time we revisit the conversation". The "conversation" for those not in the know is the talk that black parents have with their kids as it relates to how to safely interact with the police. The reasons why we have these conversations are based on personal experiences and the fact that statistically speaking, black people experience more negative interactions with the police than white people, taking into account the relative numbers of each population.

I looked at Jada and asked her if she remembered having the "police conversation" from last year. She said, "Yes, I remember." I asked her if she remembered why we had the conversation. Jada responded, "Because those police officers pulled up next to you at the red light and started looking at you and then they slowed down after the light turned green, got behind your car and followed us until we got to the restaurant."

To give you some perspective, sometime in June of 2019, Tiffany, Jada and I were driving through Kirkwood, Missouri, because we were going to meet my close friend, Shay, her boyfriend, Wade, and Shay's daughter, Elise, for dinner at a restaurant at 7:00 PM. True confession. I have to admit the driving through Kirkwood in the evening hours is a bit traumatic for me because I grew up being told Kirkwood, like many parts of South County St. Louis, were off-limits to black people after dark due to the city's history of racial harassment of people of color.

So, there we were driving through Kirkwood at 6:50 P.M. and I hear Google maps say we are less than six minutes away from our destination. We were sitting at a red light and a police car with two police officers inside, pulled up next to me. I looked over and I happened to notice that both officers were staring at me. I gave a polite nod and then looked over to my wife who was completely aware of the situation, as she is always aware of everything that's happening. Tiffany said, "I'm glad we're close to the restaurant because those cops are staring at you like they know you or something."

This was her attempt at humor in order to calm me and Jada down. The light turned green and I proceeded to drive ahead. At this point, the police officer slowed down and angled his police vehicle behind mine. I made a right down the street and the officer also turned, right behind me. Maybe 30 seconds later, I made a left and they did the same.

I was trying to act in a calm manner because I did not want to alarm Jada, but my daughter is a pretty sharp cookie. She asked, "Daddy are the cops following us? They keep turning everywhere we turn." Tiffany said, "Yes, they are following us, but I'm going to need you to stay calm Jada. Can you do that for me?" Jada nodded her head, but I could see the nervousness creep across her face as I looked in the rear-view mirror. Then I said, "Jada, let's go over some things, okay? The police are following us even though I'm driving the speed limit and I've done nothing wrong. In the event that we do get pulled over, I want you to keep your seatbelt on and you are to look forward. I do not want you to look at the cop when he comes to my window, just focus on the back of my head. Okay?" She said, "Yes, sir."

"If the cop does pull us over. I'm going to pull my license and registration out and put it on the dashboard before he comes to the window. I will keep my hands on the steering wheel and Tiffany will sit in her seat with both hands flat on her thighs. I need you to do the same as Tiffany, Jada. If the cop pulls me out of the car, you are not to react nor will you look out the window, okay? I want you to focus all of your attention on Tiffany, not me. You will not react if you see the police officer putting handcuffs on me or you hear me screaming. Do you understand?"

Jada said, "But daddy, I'm not going to let them hurt you." I said, "Jada, I don't matter. I do not matter. What matters is that you and Tiffany are safe. There's nothing you can do if the police hurt me because I'd rather them hurt me than to hurt you and Tiffany, do you understand?" Jada said, "Daddy..." and I immediately cut her off by asking in a firm voice, "Do you understand?" She gave a reluctant, "Yes, sir," but I could hear the pain in her voice.

We finally pulled into the parking lot of the restaurant. The police slowly drove past us, while looking at my car and they drove away. Keep in mind that this entire event unfolded over the course of five minutes, but five minutes felt like five hours. We all took a collective deep breath. I looked at Tiffany as she returned my gaze. There's something to be said for having a shared experience, because we didn't have to say anything at all, but our eyes conveyed an entire conversation full of hurt, pain and fear.

We stepped out of the car and we gave Jada a huge hug because she was clearly shaken up. We told her that "We're safe. We're going to go into this restaurant, eat some good food and we're going to have fun."

We met Shay and her family in the restaurant and proceeded to tell them about what transpired. Shay and Wade, both of whom are white, are about as open-minded as two people can possibly be. It was comforting talking with them because they didn't attempt to "white-splain" away the officer's actions with questions such as, "Well, were you speeding? Did you stop at the light correctly? What did you do to make the police officer follow you?" This is what we normally hear from our white associates who attempt to pin the blame on us as a means of exonerating the actions of the police officers because, of course, we're the ones to blame, not the police.

Getting back to the evening of June 5th, I was pleasantly surprised at how much Jada remembered about the events that took place last year. Considering the fact that she's 14, she's less than two years away from getting her driver's license. We took her through multiple scenarios in which she gets pulled over by the police, because we wanted to ensure that she knew how to respond to the officers because all that matters is, that she gets home safely.

The conversation evolved into the current social and racial unrest. Jada shared with us how shocked and amazed she was about the level of activism from her school classmates, but she felt a bit embarrassed because she had little knowledge about Floyd and the protests and riots because no one had really talked to her about it. We agreed that we would watch the George Floyd video so that she would have some perspective.

That's how come, on June 7th, we were all sitting in front of my computer. We pulled up the video. It's one thing to watch the video by yourself or with your spouse. It's another thing to watch it with your 14-year-old daughter who's trying to process all of this. When Floyd uttered, "I can't breathe" Jada reacted to the video as though it was happening in real time. She was crying and she said to the officer, "Get off his neck, get off his neck." As he said again, "I can't breathe," I saw Jada crying and rocking back and forth in her seat. She dropped her head when Floyd screamed, "Mama."

As the video came to a close, I hugged Jada and asked her if she was okay. She looked up at me and screamed, "Why do they hate us, daddy? Why do they hate us? He killed that man. Why do they hate us?" I said, "They don't all hate us, Jada." She responded with, "But then why did he kill that man? Because he was black?"

As a diversity trainer, I'm paid to educate people on all aspects of diversity and yet I was speechless when my daughter asked, "why do they hate us, Daddy?" There was nothing more humbling than searching for the right words to say to my daughter as she struggled with the thought of people hating her. I helped to bring this child into the world with the hope that I could give her a better life than I ever had; with the hope that she will not have to go through the things that I went through; with the hope that she will never have to experience cross burnings and having urine thrown in her face; with the hope that she will never be called nigger.

The only thing I could do was hold her tight and press her head against my chest. I said to her, "I don't know why people hate us, but I know that we love you and I know that we will always do our best to keep you safe. We will always do our best to make sure that you see another day."

At this point, Tiffany turned up the sound to videos of Black Lives Matter protests that are occurring around the world. She wanted Jada to hear people chanting, "Black Lives Matter." Jada looked at the screen and asked, "What is this?" Tiffany said, "Jada, after George Floyd was murdered, there were protests happening around the world of people marching in the streets chanting, 'Black Lives Matter.' People are standing up for your life, for our lives. We can't tell you why Chauvin did what he did to George Floyd, but we can tell you, people are standing up because they know your life matters. People are standing up for you."

We hugged Jada. In that moment there were three black people, hoping and praying that our lives do matter. After we broke our embrace, Jada looked at me and said, "Daddy, George Floyd could have been you. Tiffany, that could have been you on the street and there was nothing that I could have done to protect you." I didn't know what to say to her...again.

> If you are a person of color, when did you have that conversation with your child? If you are white, did you ever imagine it necessary to have such a conversation?

Fail Fast...And Learn From Your Mistakes

At some time, you are going to say or do the wrong thing; it is inevitable, and it happens to everyone. Perhaps you will say something that is culturally inappropriate without realizing that you really stepped in it or you go overboard trying to prove your worth as an ally, with little comprehension of the fact that you are coming across as unintentionally condescending. Guess what? It happens to the best of us. The key is to be open if/when the mistake is brought to your attention, learn from it and pledge to do better in the future. In other words, fail fast and learn from your mistakes.

Let me describe an example of this. On June 29, 2020 my friend Bonny, who happens to be white, reached out to me out of concern for her 15-year-old grandson, John. When John was 12, a group of boys convinced him to say "nigger" during a sleepover at his grandparent's house. What John did not know was that one of the boys was recording him on his cellphone and then proceeded to upload the video to a social media site. Within a matter of minutes, this young man was bombarded by comments ranging from "you're a racist" to threats of bodily harm. The threats died down over time and John assumed that people would forget about the video.

Unfortunately, the video resurfaced in the wake of the social unrest caused by George Floyd's murder. John, who is now a freshman in high school, was being taunted for being racist as a result of the video. This caused a great deal of frustration for John and his grandparents because he wanted so badly to tell everyone in his high school that he is not a racist, but no one was willing to listen to him when the video clearly showed him saying "nigger" at least three times. Not only was John dealing with the stigma of being branded a racist, he is also physically smaller than the other kids and has experienced his fair share of other people's nasty behavior.

Bonny asked me if I would be willing to speak to John with the hope that I could help him navigate through the complexities that he was facing in addition to having an open discussion about the current state of race relations in this country. In all candor, I agreed to speak with John because Bonny is my friend but I had grown increasingly frustrated with my white friends asking me to speak to them about race only to have everything I put in front of them challenged and dismissed as though racism was nothing more than a media created tool to divide the races. If I experienced this with adults, then I could only imagine how badly this was going to be dealing with a 15-year-old.

We arranged to meet via Zoom, and I was 15 minutes late for the video call because I was dealing with clients, so I came into the call with the attitude of "okay, let's get this over with." Bonny and John appeared, and I was blown away by how charming John was. I asked him to tell me what happened, and John recounted everything that led up to him saying "nigger" on video, including the fact that he filmed an apology video taking ownership for his mistake with a vow to learn and be better in the future. During our conversation, he kept referring to "nigger" as the "n-word". I asked him to say the word, more as a test than anything else because I wanted to see if he was truly sorry for using the word or sorry that he got caught. John refused to say the word, even as I gently prodded him to say it. I asked him, "Why the reluctance to say "nigger"? You clearly said it in the video. What's the difference now?" John said, "I didn't know what the n-word meant. I heard it in rap music, and I've heard my father use it a number of times, but I still didn't understand the disgusting history of the word until I started doing my own research. I hate that word and I hate how it has been used against black people."

Another wrinkle for John is that his father, who is white, lives in a predominately African American neighborhood and is often very friendly with his neighbors but routinely refers to blacks as niggers and other derogatory terms. John said, "I don't understand it. I've seen him talking to the black people in his neighborhood. He jokes with them and it seems like they're friends, but he is always calling them the 'n-word' when he's not around them." John went on to say, "My father's family is racist. They're always saying ignorant stuff about black people. I don't understand it. Me and three of my cousins hate it. I just wish they would change but I'm not sure how to make them change. I don't like it."

Over the course of our conversation, John went into greater detail on what he's learned about race relations in America. He literally educated me and his grandmother on everything from "white privilege" to the way minorities have been unequally treated in America. I was so blown away by his knowledge and the confidence in which he spoke that I offered him a job with my company as soon as he graduates from high school!

John is a prime example of failing fast and learning from your mistakes along the way.

> Think back to when you have or said something, and then regretted it, either at the time or very soon after? How long did it take for you to rectify the situation? What did you do to make up for it?

Pain

Towards the end of June, Phil & Jason were in conversation. Amongst other things, they were talking about what were black people's fears. Jason described a fear he had been experiencing in recent weeks.

"My life has been defined by the pain of racism. The thought of actually being in a post-racial society, scares me. I don't know how to live without the pain of racism."

c) Today's Reality

Jason's is not an isolated story; in this section we have endeavored to present objective, research-based statistics on just one aspect of racism and discrimination – incarceration and policing. In any scientific endeavor, it is often difficult to get to a widely agreed upon, set of data. This becomes even more difficult with the topics of racism and discrimination as there has been pitifully little research and data collection carried out. In a recent article in Nature, Tracey Meares, founding director of the Justice Collaboratory at Yale Law School, referring to data concerning racial bias and the use of force, states the following:

"Most agencies do not collect that data in a systematic way."

She goes on to say:

"Policing, in large part for political reasons, has proceeded in kind of a science-free zone."

In researching this book, we could not find a single, centralized, complete, and accurate source of all police killings, let alone one that addresses all sources of racism and discrimination. The closest we could find was the Washington Post's database. The Washington Post is compiling a database of every fatal shooting in the United States by a police officer in the line of duty since Jan. 1, 2015. Where available they record the race of the deceased, the circumstances of the shooting, whether the person was armed and whether the victim was experiencing a mental-health crisis. They collect the data anecdotally by culling local news reports, law enforcement websites and social media and by monitoring independent databases.

We recognize, therefore, that any set of statistics needs to be viewed with care. Nevertheless, we felt that some of the numbers that are available, are worth reviewing; but a word of warning. The data are quite stark. And our data just covers policing and the judicial system. Our research indicates that the data are similar in almost every institutional aspect of American life, whether it be health care, banking or housing.

- The fatality rate for police shootings is 2.8 times higher among blacks than whites.

- White officers dispatched to black neighborhoods fired their guns five times as often as black officers dispatched for similar calls to the same neighborhoods. [6]

- Black and white Americans sell and use drugs at similar rates, but black Americans are 2.7 times as likely to be arrested for drug-related offenses. [7]

- At the state level, Blacks are about 6.5 times as likely as whites to be incarcerated for the same drug-related crimes. [8]

- In twelve states, more than half of the prison population is black: Alabama, Delaware, Georgia, Illinois, Louisiana, Maryland, Michigan, Mississippi, New Jersey, North Carolina, South Carolina, and Virginia. Maryland, whose prison population is 72% African American, tops the nation. [12] Blacks represent far less than 50% of the population in each of these states.

- In Oklahoma, the state with the highest overall black incarceration rate, 1 in 15 black males ages 18 and older is in prison. [12]

- Majorities of both black and white Americans say black people are treated less fairly than whites in dealing with the police and by the criminal justice system as a whole. In a 2019 Pew Research Center survey, 84% of black adults said that, in dealing with police, blacks are generally treated less fairly than whites; 63% of whites said the same. Similarly, 87% of blacks and 61% of whites said the U.S. criminal justice system treats black people less fairly. [9]

- Black adults are about five times as likely as whites to say they've been unfairly stopped by police because of their race or ethnicity (44% vs. 9%), according to the same survey. Black men are especially likely to say this: 59% say they've been unfairly stopped, versus 31% of black women. [14]

- Nearly two-thirds of black adults (65%) say they've been in situations where people acted as if they were suspicious of them because of their race or ethnicity, while only a quarter of white adults say that's happened to them. Roughly a third of both Asian and Hispanic adults (34% and 37%, respectively) say they've been in such situations, the 2019 survey found. [14]

- Black Americans are far less likely than whites to give police high marks for the way they do their jobs. In a 2016 survey, only about a third of black adults said that police in their community did an "excellent" or "good" job in using the right amount of force (33%, compared with 75% of whites), treating racial and ethnic groups equally (35% vs. 75%) and holding officers accountable for misconduct (31% vs. 70%). [14]

➤ In the past, police officers and the general public have tended to view fatal encounters between black people and police very differently. In a 2016 survey of nearly 8,000 policemen and women from departments with at least 100 officers, two-thirds said most such encounters are isolated incidents and not signs of broader problems between police and the black community. In a companion survey of more than 4,500 U.S. adults, 60% of the public called such incidents signs of broader problems between police and black people. But the views given by police themselves were sharply differentiated by race: A majority of black officers (57%) said that such incidents were evidence of a broader problem, but only 27% of white officers and 26% of Hispanic officers said so. [14]

➤ White police officers and their black colleagues have starkly different views on fundamental questions regarding the situation of blacks in American society, the 2016 survey found. For example, nearly all white officers (92%) – but only 29% of their black colleagues – said the U.S. had made the changes needed to assure equal rights for blacks. [14]

➤ An overwhelming majority of police officers (86%) said in 2016 that high profile fatal encounters between black people and police officers had made their jobs harder. Sizable majorities also said such incidents had made their colleagues more worried about safety (93%), heightened tensions between police and blacks (75%), and left many officers reluctant to use force when appropriate (76%) or to question people who seemed suspicious (72%). [14]

But maybe there's hope:

➤ The nation's imprisonment rate is at its lowest level in more than two decades. The greatest decline has come among black Americans, whose imprisonment rate has decreased 34% since 2006. [10]

Part 2: Some headlines:

The purpose of the second part of this section on Today's Reality is to present some news stories that were current at the time of writing this book, to show that the topics we are discussing are not things of the past; there is still significant discrimination and racism today. These cover approximately a one-week period.

A restaurant denied service to a Black boy for his clothes, but video shows a White boy, dressed similarly, was allowed in.
(Alicia Lee, CNN, June 24, 2020)

A Baltimore restaurant group has apologized after a video showed a black woman and her son being denied service because the boy's clothes didn't fit the restaurant's dress code, even though a white boy, dressed similarly, was seemingly allowed to dine there.

On Monday, Marcia Grant, the boy's mother, posted videos to her social media channels of the Ouzo Bay restaurant denying her and her son service because he was wearing athletic shorts.

"So we want to eat and they're telling me my son can't eat here because there's no athletic wear. He's 9. And there's kids out there with tennis shoes on," Grant can be heard saying in the video, which shows her son wearing black tennis shoes, athletic shorts and a t-shirt.

"Unfortunately, we do have a dress code," the restaurant employee says as he suggests that the boy possibly change into "nonathletic shorts."

Grant then turns the camera to outside the restaurant where a white boy, who, according to Grant, "just ate here," can be seen wearing tennis shoes and a t-shirt. The employee goes on to say that based on what his boss told them while tennis shoes are allowed, athletic shorts and shirts aren't, and he claims that the white boy's shirt isn't what the restaurant would classify as an athletic shirt.

Police Officer Fired for Saying He 'Can't Wait' to Slaughter Black People
(Khaleda Rahman, Newseek, June 25, 2020)

A North Carolina police officer (We will refer to him as "Officer A)" has been fired after being caught on camera saying he "can't wait" to slaughter black people and that a civil war was needed to wipe them out.

At one point, Officer A says he knew another officer was "bad news" and added: "Let's see how his boys take care of him when sh** gets rough, see if they don't put a bullet in his head."

Around 30 minutes later, Officer A received a phone call from Officer B, according to the investigation. During that conversation, Officer B, referred to a black woman he had arrested the day before as a "negro" and a racial slur, multiple times. "She needed a bullet in her head right then and move on," Officer B, also said about the woman, according to the investigative documents.

Officer B, also described a black magistrate as a "f****** negro magistrate."

Later, Officer A, told Officer B that he feels a civil war is coming and that he is "ready." Officer A, said he was going to buy a new assault rifle, and soon "we are just going to go out and start slaughtering them f****** n******. I can't wait. God, I can't wait."

Officer B, responded that he wouldn't do that, but Officer A, said: "I'm ready." Officer A, then told Officer B, that he felt a civil war was needed to "wipe 'em off the f****** map. That'll put them back about four or five generations." Officer B, told Officer A, he was "crazy."

According to police, the officers admitted it was their voices on the video and didn't deny any of the things said. All three denied they were racists and they blamed their comments on the stress on working in law enforcement amid protests sparked by the death of George Floyd.

Former Police Officers 'Openly Plotting' To Kill BLM Activist Shaun King
(Soo Kim, Newseek, June 26, 2020)

An investigation has been launched after members of a Facebook group for California law enforcement officers were found to be allegedly planning to kill Shaun King, an activist for the Black Lives Matter movement and other social causes.

Mississippi pastor says he was kicked out of church for saying 'black lives matter'
(Caleb Parke, Fox News, June 26, 2020)

A Columbus, Miss., pastor, who is white, was given the boot by his former church for supporting protests and the idea that "black lives matter" after George Floyd's police-related death.

A biracial woman says she was set on fire in Wisconsin. Authorities are now investigating the incident as a hate crime
(Amir Vera, Jaide Timm-Garcia and Raja Razek, CNN, June 27, 2020)

Madison police and the FBI have launched a hate crime investigation after an 18-year-old biracial woman was set on fire.

The assault took place early Wednesday morning when the woman was driving and stopped at a red light and "heard someone yell out a racial epithet," according to a police incident report.

The woman is not named in the report, but a family spokesperson identified her as Althea Bernstein, a college student and a volunteer EMT.

"She looked and saw four men, all white. She says one used a spray bottle to deploy a liquid on her face and neck, and then threw a flaming lighter at her, causing the liquid to ignite," read the report, which was filed over the phone.

Being black in business is being 'on your own'
(Samira Hussain & Natalie Sherman, BBC News, New York, June 28, 2020)

Pam Brown and her husband Christopher know they will need help if the yoga studio they own in New York is going to survive the pandemic.

But they don't think they will get it, at least not from the government. The reason? They're black.

As Ms Brown says: "Being a black business owner is really being out on your own."

The Browns, who founded their Align Brooklyn studio in 2014, applied for low-cost government loans offered as part of the trillions of dollars the US government has spent to help business.

But although they received some funds to help cover wages for their staff, their other applications were rejected.

Ms Brown hasn't been told why, but she suspects the value of their assets to act as security for loans - a category that would include homes or other investments - weren't substantial enough to qualify.

"We've done an exceptional job running our business," she says. "And I think that when the evaluation comes down to having a basis of wealth - having a house, having a lot of money in the bank to be able to sustain something like this - it's just obviously going to impact African American people significantly more."

On the face it, giving loans to people based on the size of their assets is not racial discrimination.

But the net worth of the typical black family in the US was $17,150 in 2016 - one-tenth that of whites, according to the Brookings Institution. That means it's almost inevitable that black small businesses like the Browns are less likely to get the government lifeline of a loan, than their white counterparts.

"The key problem here is a lot of African American-owned, Latin American-owned, immigrant-owned businesses - they don't have a lot of capital," says economist Robert Fairlie, a professor at the University of California, Santa Cruz. "How long can you last dipping into your savings, when you're starting at a point that's so low?"

Alabama mayor resigns after post about Crimson Tide's BLM video
Associated Press, June 28, 2020

CARBON HILL, ALA. -- A controversial Alabama mayor has resigned after posting disparaging comments about the University of Alabama football team voicing its support for the Black Lives Matter movement.

Carbon Hill Mayor Mark Chambers submitted his resignation letter to the city clerk on Saturday, news outlets reported. The town council hasn't approved it yet, but an emergency meeting will be held Wednesday.

A Facebook post from Chambers on Saturday said he was selling his photos of the Alabama football team and head coach Nick Saban because of their "sorry" political views. He said "the Tide is done in my opinion."

In a video shared by Alabama football, Saban and players read an essay by Crimson Tide offensive lineman Alex Leatherwood, who wrote, "All lives can't matter until Black lives matter."

Chambers previously faced scrutiny last year for complaining on social media about "baby killers" and "socialists," saying "homosexuals lecture us on morals" and "transvestites lecture us on human biology."

Chambers wrote: "The only way to change it would be to kill the problem out." Chambers initially denied the comment but later apologized. Two town council members later resigned, reportedly because they didn't want to be associated with his comments.

Carbon Hill is located outside Birmingham and has about 2,000 residents.

Woman Yells 'You Live Off White People' in Racist Rant at BLM Protesters
(Seren Morris, Newsweek, June 30, 2020)

A woman in Pennsylvania shouted racist abuse at Black Lives Matter protesters on Sunday and told them, "You live off white people."

As the protesters in Watsontown chanted "No justice, no peace," the white woman shouted "trash" and "f*** you, we're going to give you no peace."

A protester can be heard off camera shouting "We love you" as the woman says "b****, f****** b****." She shouts at the protesters, "You live off of white people" and they again reply with "We love you," to which she responds: "you f****** communists" and "f*** off, keep your HIV over there."

Wrongly arrested Black man said he knew he was going to be falsely accused as police approached him

(Madeline Holcombe, Tina Burnside and Pierre Meilhan, CNN, June 30, 2020)

As Valdosta police approached Antonio Smith, he was terrified and thought he was going to "get pinned for something I didn't do," he told CNN.

"Oh my God, it's one of these days where they are going to probably arrest me, and take me off, and probably won't find me anymore," Smith said he was thinking as officers approached him in that February incident, he told CNN's Chris Cuomo Monday.

Smith, a black man, is suing the Georgia city of Valdosta and numerous Valdosta Police Department officers for excessive force and for violating his civil rights after he was slammed to the ground as he was wrongly arrested.

A 911 call, a racial slur, a refusal to cash a check. This is what it's like for some Black bank customers

(Faith Karimi. CNN, July 2, 2020)

Paul McCowns walked into an Ohio bank clutching his first paycheck from a new job at an electric company. But instead of cashing the check worth about $1,000, the teller called 911.

As he walked out of the Huntington Bank branch in Brooklyn empty-handed, an officer waiting outside handcuffed him and put him in the back of a police cruiser.

"I have a customer here -- he's not our customer, actually. He's trying to cash a check and the check is fraudulent. It does not match our records," a bank employee says on a recording of the 911 call obtained by CNN.

For many African Americans, what happened to McCowns in December 2018 is a common experience. Banking while Black is another entry in an ever-growing list of people calling the police on African Americans doing everyday things.

No data exists on how prevalent the issue is, but such cases have made headlines in recent years. Florida civil rights attorney <u>Yechezkel Rodal said</u> he gets calls from Black people all over the nation after his client sued a bank two years ago. Some incidents end in lawsuits or private settlements with the banks -- but many more occur in financial institutions big and small with no repercussions, he said.

But, as we said in the previous section, maybe there's hope:

Black D.C. archbishop's rise marks a historic moment

(Elana Schor. Associated Press, Oct 25, 2020)

Washington D.C. Archbishop Wilton Gregory is set to become the first Black U.S. prelate to assume the rank of cardinal in the Catholic Church, a historic appointment that comes months after nationwide demonstrations against racial injustice.

Gregory's ascension, announced on Sunday by Pope Francis alongside 12 other newly named cardinals, elevates a leader who has drawn praise for his handling of the sexual abuse scandal that has roiled the church. The Washington-area archbishop also has spoken out in recent days about the importance of Catholic leaders working to combat the sin of racial discrimination.

The 72-year-old Gregory, ordained in his native Chicago in 1973, took over leadership of the capital's archdiocese last year after serving as archbishop of Atlanta since 2005. The ceremony making his elevation official is slated for Nov. 28.

"With a very grateful and humble heart, I thank Pope Francis for this appointment which will allow me to work more closely with him in caring for Christ's Church," Gregory said in a statement issued by the archdiocese.

Chapter Three:
An Introduction to the Brain

Police Violence

Discrimination

Racial Slurs and Insults

Police Deaths

Racial Profiling

Public Violence

Public Deaths

Death Threats

Redlining

Healthcare

Recruiting
Biases

Micro
Injuries

False Imprisonment

Wealth Inequality

Educational Discrimination

Mass
Incarceration

Racial PTSD and Trauma

An Introduction to the Brain

It is difficult to follow these heart-tugging stories and move to an objective, scientific discussion of the brain; but, our belief is that if we can help to explain what is going on in our brains, then we can provide a platform upon which we can build a process to move forward. If you prefer to jump straight to what we should be doing, and skip some of these more detailed explanations, then now would be a good time to move ahead to the last part of the book, page 141.

When Phil gives presentations and lectures, he will often tell people that he is going to give them an excuse that will serve them for the rest of their lives. He suggests that they say, "It was not me; it was my brain!" Most people laugh, but it gives them an opportunity to look at their brain (hence their thoughts, reactions and behavior) from the point of view of a third-party. It is easier to be objective that way. And that is what we are proposing here. If we can understand our brains in an objective manner, then we can respond in one of two ways. We can either give ourselves some degree of freedom to step back, reflect and maybe adopt some changes; or we can use our new knowledge to justify our actions and stay exactly where we are. Clearly, we hope for the former.

a) How the Brain Works [d]

Our brains are incredible. We won't go into all of the details, but they are immensely complicated, handling vast amounts of information every second – most of it beneath our conscious awareness.

Unfortunately, however, they were designed to be perfectly functional for the situation they found themselves in many millions of years ago. They were designed (or more accurately, evolved) to do one thing – to ensure your survival. That is the brain's primary purpose. And they did a great job when we were all trying to eke an existence during pre-historic times; after all, humankind survived to be where we are in 2020!

---

[d] This is a drastic simplification; for anyone wishing to go into more detail, there are plenty of books available – including our own.

Fast forward to today, and we find ourselves dealing with modern day problems – using ancient brain technology! Brain 2.0 hasn't yet been developed. Our ancient brains are ill-equipped for today's societal environment and, as you will come to see, this ancient brain is a significant contributor to the problems that we face today. Yet that's what we have, so it's best to understand how our brains function and the impact of that functioning.

At its most basic, the brain consists of two parts – which, for the sake of simplicity, we will call the <u>emotional</u> brain and the <u>logical</u> brain. They are in a constant dialog, and an occasional struggle, with one another. The emotional brain reacts quickly and is driven by instinct, biases and habits. On the other hand, the logical brain is rational, thoughtful, significantly more evolved, and is able to put moment-to-moment events into context but is slower than the emotional brain.

Let's examine the emotional brain first. Tom Rieger in his recent book [11], *Curing Organizational Blindness*, describes the emotional brain as follows:

> *"The emotional brain is automatic. It is very deeply ingrained in our evolutionary psychology, running through your body's emotional central processor. It seeks simplicity and assigns cause and effect. It becomes awash in adrenaline and other bio-chemicals when under stress. It is the home of deep instinctive beliefs and is always at the ready."*

This emotional brain is like *"the sentry at his or her post, after ten really strong cups of espresso."* It is constantly scanning its environment on the lookout for things which might threaten you.

In addition, the processes of the emotional brain are automatic, appear effortless, are difficult to control and difficult to modify.

Now a quick glimpse into the rational brain:

> *" … the more rational brain is responsible for things like doubt, reason, deep concentration, complex mental tasks and calculations, choice, and "agency" or self-*

82

control. It resides in the more intellectual, and more recently evolved, pre-frontal cortex… the logic center of the brain."

The operations of the rational or logical brain are slower, serial in nature, require effort, yet can be deliberately controlled, are flexible and governed by learned rules.

It also turns out that the logical brain is very easily distracted, gets tired very easily and is significantly impacted by stress.

Between them, these two parts of our brain drive almost everything we think and every response we have, so it is very worthwhile to understand them. And how they work, or don't work, together.

We stated earlier that the brain has one main purpose. To ensure your survival. The emotional brain really takes that task to heart! [e] It constantly scans its environment looking for threats and rewards. In fact, it does so every one fifth of a second. While it does look for both threats <u>and</u> for rewards, it is primed for, and is always on the alert for, threats. The brain has five times as many neural circuits to look for threats as it does for reward. We are geared towards responding to threat. When the sentry sees a threat, it wants to react rapidly, and is largely driven by instinct, biases and habits.

Ideally, we need both parts of our brains to work in concert, with both of them being at full capacity. This will enable us to make better decisions and choices overall. When it is working perfectly, when the sentry detects a threat, before it actually acts, it sends a check-in message to the logical part of the brain, for it to perform a brief analysis. Is this an actual threat? The logical brain, analyzes the threat and refers to what it knows about the context etc. It then sends a message back to the sentry either confirming the threat or saying that there really is no threat! The equivalent of telling the sentry to stand down. Researchers call the logical part "The brain's braking mechanism"

But as Tom points out:

"… when it comes to decision-making, there is a critical challenge of getting both parts of the brain to stay in their respective lanes of expertise, and at the same time, work together."

---

[e] Yes we know. We are mixing metaphors.

"The emotional brain arrives at conclusions first, often with incomplete information, and backfills arguments based on experience, emotion, and context. It also assures us that we can and should "trust our gut" and rely on "intuition" for all kinds of decisions, not just instinct-driven reactions that come from our need to survive. The speed of the emotional brain makes our gut feelings the default setting for decision making, rather than the careful and cautious thought processes of the rational brain."

"That's not so bad for trivial or minor decisions. But it gets complicated when the stakes are high. In those cases, research suggests that when the rewards can be substantial, the emotional brain over-emphasizes the upside, and downplays the risks. That makes us vulnerable to making an overly risky decision, perhaps at the expense of a better one."

"Conversely, our emotional brain also magnifies temporary and short-term losses over long-term gains, amplifying the sense of risk and loss."

Let's pause a moment and summarize what we have learned so far. We have two parts to the brain; a hypervigilant, caffeine-driven sentry tracking everything that might be a threat or a reward and ready to react in a split second's notice. And a laid-back thinker that can provide rational explanations and contextual meaning to any given event, but that gets tired, stressed and easily distracted.

> Take a minute and think back to Jason's stories. For Jason, when do you think the emotional part of his brain was in control, and when do you think the rational part was in control? What about for some of the other people involved. What about the kids at Valparaiso that wanted to touch his hair? Which part of their brains, the rational or the emotional was driving them? Have any experiences conditioned you to always be at or near a threat state?

Let's dig a little deeper into what's going on with this 'sentry' and what it is on the lookout for. The threats that we face these days are no longer being attacked by a saber-toothed tiger on the way back to our cave. Nowadays, the threats are more likely to be the traffic on the way home, the impending deadline on a project, the scowl that the boss made when we arrived at work or some of the fears that we all have about COVID-19. But, unfortunately, the brain doesn't know the difference between a real physical threat and a perceived 'social or emotional threat.' The brain treats social or emotional threats in a very similar manner to how it treats physical threats. To the brain they are handled by similar neural circuitry and the brain reacts to both types of threat in the same way. The brain 'buckets' threats into three broad categories.

The first bucket concerns our need to feel Protected.

> ➢ We want to know that we are safe.
> ➢ We want to feel physically safe, emotionally safe and financially safe.
> ➢ We want to be treated fairly.
> ➢ We want to know where we stand.

The second bucket is our need for Participation.

> ➢ We are social animals, and, to a large degree, we enjoy interaction with others.
> ➢ We want to know that we are accepted into, and approved by, our group – especially a group of people that are important to us.
> ➢ We want to know that our voice is heard, and our opinions taken into account.
> ➢ We want to avoid looking stupid in front of our family, friends and peers.

The third of the buckets is Prediction.

> ➢ Our brains want to know what is going to happen next.
> ➢ We want to have some sense of control over our lives.
> ➢ We want to know what is expected of us.
> ➢ We want to know what is going on.

As we stated earlier, in addition to looking for threats, the sentry is also looking for rewards. Once it is satisfied that there are no threats, it can deal with rewards. It divides these rewards into two more buckets. Purpose and Pleasure.

Purpose

> ➢ We want mastery in our fields and have an opportunity to practice it.
> ➢ We want to develop ourselves/self-actualize.
> ➢ We want to know that our lives have Meaning.
> ➢ We want to live in accordance with our core values and work with people/organizations that align with those values.
> ➢ We want to be able to express ourselves artistically.

- ➤ We want to explore our spirituality.
- ➤ We want to feel passionate about something
- ➤ We want to have a challenge.
- ➤ We want to seek the truth.

Pleasure

- ➤ We want to experience joy and happiness.
- ➤ We want to experience sensual gratification.
- ➤ We want to experience instant gratification.
- ➤ We want to experience stimulation and excitement.
- ➤ We want to play.
- ➤ We want to be loved.

> Think back to some of the stakeholders in Jason's stories. What type of threats did they perceive in Jason? What threats did Jason see in them? Was Jason's brain ever really in a reward state – was there ever a time when he had no sense of feeling threatened?

In the next several chapters, we will explore the three threat categories in a lot more detail. We have included the detailed descriptions of the components of the five categories in Appendix A. Take a look through and see which of them apply to you.

Finally, there is another really important manner in which the brain operates that impacts everything that we do. Literally everything. The brain operates in two modes – a conscious mode, where we are aware of what is happening, and a nonconscious mode, which is going on 'behind the curtain.' This may come as a surprise to you but, we are mainly driven by the nonconscious part of our brain. It drives most of our decisions and reactions.

So, when the over-caffeinated sentry makes a decision without the benefit of his or her logical counterpart, it is likely to be happening behind the scenes. But wait. It gets worse. The ratio between what goes on nonconsciously behind the scenes and what goes on in our conscious awareness, is about a million to one. Far more decisions, even important ones, are happening in the nonconscious mode. When the logical part of the brain is inhibited from providing a 'controlling influence' over the emotional brain, the emotional brain gets to completely run the show!

Some examples of things that will inhibit the logical brain are stress, exhaustion (mental, physical or emotional), lack of sleep, juggling too many tasks, time pressures, and having made too many decisions or overrides of the emotional brain already that day! This logical part of the brain is the center of social control – it has the ability to suppress urges that, if not suppressed, could lead to socially unacceptable outcomes.

Unfortunately, the dynamics that inhibit the logical brain are all things that are part and parcel of almost every environment that we find ourselves in these days.

Let's take a look at one of them in more detail; stress. Let's look at what happens when the sentry perceives a threat. It gets the brain geared up and ready to respond. By a complex mechanism which we don't need to go into, it sends chemical messages to the logical part of the brain, telling it that its influence is not needed. And the sentry springs into action getting the body prepared to fight or flee. This made great sense when the main threat was a physical one and the need for survival was paramount. If the logical part of the brain decided to put everything on hold for even a second while it considered the context, then you were likely to be some large animal's lunch. Speed was of the essence, and the emotional brain's rapid-response mechanism was perfectly designed for the job.

In the more complex environment of today, where many of the threats are social and emotional, and are way more nuanced, then allowing the emotional brain to run the show, may not be optimal.

Once again, let's pause a moment and summarize what we just said. If the sentry perceives a threat, it turns off its logical counterpart and starts running the show on its own. Wait! What? That means all the rational, context-based analysis and self-control processes that the, albeit slower, logical part of the brain brings to the table, are no longer available. The brain is now being driven by our caffeine-stoked sentry!

Even when we are not stressed, our decisions are very often highly influenced by our emotional brain, rather than the logical one. Under threat i.e. when we are stressed, we all tend to make even less rational decisions.

Moving on, and we hate to tell you this, but the story of the brain is about to get even worse. There are several other dynamics which influence us on a moment by moment basis.

First, our brains are driven by biases, habits and on-going patterns of behavior, much of which is happening behind the scenes i.e. at the nonconscious level. Some of these biases are innate and have been with us for a while, for evolutionary reasons. Some of them are unique to each of us. We will examine these in much more detail in the next section.

> In the meantime, review Jason's stories again, and describe what biases you can identify. To what degree were the impact of those biases influenced by stress?

Second, our brains hate change. The brain develops models for everything that it has to deal with, whether that is the concept of voting, or a banana, or our favorite uncle. Once it has these models, it does not like to revise them. If new data come along that fit into our existing models, our brain accepts the data and integrates it. If the new data does not fit, then, at best, it causes the brain to resist the change – at worst, it causes our brain to selectively ignore the information that is not consistent with our model. The issue of change and the brain is so important that we devote a section to it later.

> What mental models did the protagonists that burned the crosses in Jason and Jerome's story, have of black people? What mental model are Tiffany and Jason creating of the police in Jada's mind?

Third, despite our wonderful brains and the incredible power that they have, even at the best of times, we will often behave irrationally. There are a number of reasons for this. For example, we may behave irrationally if:

- ➢ we see something that is unfair, either to us or to other people.
- ➢ specific words or metaphors are used.
- ➢ something is framed a certain way.
- ➢ something has been "anchored" in our brain.
- ➢ we are subject to certain influences.

> Where do you see examples of irrational behavior in Jason's stories?

Fourth, the brain loves to be right. It gets a small internal 'feel-good' reward for being right. And will often distort current and past events so that it feels that it was right.

Fifth. In the absence of actual data or information, the brain will make stuff up. If there is a gap in its knowledge, it will fill in the gap with inventions of its own – and then convince itself that what it made up, is real. It convinces itself that what it invented was what actually happened. It will also use this made-up-stuff to be able to accomplish feeling right and justify actions.

> Where do you see examples of the need to feel right or making stuff up in Jason's stories?

Six. It is influenced at a nonconscious level by many things; some things impact all of us, while others are much more specific to each of us, based upon our world experience to date. Let's take two examples. First, we are influenced by someone giving us something; even if we didn't particularly want the gift, we feel a sense of obligation to give something back. Second, if we perceive something is scarce or rare, we want it more.

> What influences can you imagine were at play in some of Jason's stories?

And, number seven, emotive words significantly influence a person's thoughts and subsequent decisions. Using the words "smashed into" as opposed to "hit" will drastically alter the opinions of the listener. Adding an emotive adjective can seriously impact someone's thoughts, even though the description might be untrue. Without getting political, some recent examples of this are when COVID-19 got labelled as Kung Flu, or Hillary Clinton was given the epithet Crooked Hillary.

> What words have you heard that will have anchored in someone's mind and caused them to take a certain viewpoint with regard to racism?

Let's do a summary of what we have learned about the brain before we move on.

We have two parts to the brain, the emotional part and the logical part. The emotional part is on constant alert, ready to respond at any time. The logical part is ready to respond but more slowly. If the emotional part perceives a threat, it closes down the ability of the logical part to contribute and does its own thing. In addition, the emotional part is driven by biases, habits and patterns, does not like to change, often behaves irrationally and is subject to all sorts of other nonconscious influences.

OMG. On the face of it, this is not the best combination of traits with which to face the complex modern world. Therefore, the more we can understand what is going on in our brains, the greater the chance we can leverage the good and mitigate the not-so-good.

In his book, Tom identifies a three-part structure which explains why our brains respond the way they do. He applies this structure to the behavior within organizations, but here we are going to apply it to the wider context of individual social behavior in our communities.

The two parts of our brains approach major decisions completely differently. The speedy, emotional brain seeks to Simplify-Unify-Justify [f] to quickly arrive at a conclusion and take action. Simplify the information that is available so that it is easily digestible and aligns with our predisposed opinions and beliefs. Unify other like-minded people around us to fight for our cause. Then Justify the decision to our self and the rest of the world.

In contrast, the slower, deliberate, rational brain has the ability to approach complex issues in a more thoughtful manner. It is able to look at the issues in three parts: Understand, Plan, Address. [g] Understand the situation by evaluating all the information in a deliberate and objective manner. Plan, using various decision-making and problem-solving approaches, in order to determine what to do. Address the grievances by ensuring the voices of all stakeholders are heard and acted upon.

---

[f] Simply-Unify-Justify framework used by permission of NSI Inc. and author, Tom Rieger. All rights reserved including the right of reproduction in any form or by any means.
[g] We have adapted Tom's model to address the issue at hand

Unfortunately, without us making an explicit choice, and having motivation and discipline to do otherwise, our basic instincts will tend to adopt the Simplify-Unify-Justify approach and override a more deliberate approach.

> Take a moment and think about one of Jason's stories and reflect on what was going on in the two parts of the brain for each of the stakeholders involved.

b) Biases and Habits

Biases. We are all biased. Period. We have to be for the sake of our brain. Biases provide the brain with efficient ways to deal with the vast volume of data that is arriving second by second. Purely from the perspective of the brain, biases are useful and essential shortcuts. Biases can deal with some of the 11,000,000 bits of information that the brain is handling every second. Quick, easy, and highly energy efficient. It has worked well for us over many millennia. Biases are the brains way of not having to consciously think about everything all of the time.

While these biases have evolved for the purpose of saving energy for the brain, they are difficult for us to get our arms around. What we mean by that is this:

> ➤ We often don't believe we are biased (although we all are).
> ➤ Our biases are mostly at a nonconscious level, and so we often don't know they are there.
> ➤ Even when we know they are there, they are almost impossible to control.
> ➤ Even when we try to control them, we don't do a very good job at it.
> ➤ Trying to train ourselves out of a bias is very difficult.

Biases and habits are vitally important to the brain, to save conscious thought, and hence, energy. They are also drivers of much of our behavior, so understanding them is key. They impact everything ... our behaviors when we are on our own and when we are interacting in any way with other people, whether singly or in groups. Where we come into trouble is when we end up taking a position, holding an opinion or taking an action based on a (probably nonconscious) bias – and that position, opinion or action should have been based upon deeper and more objective considerations.

There are many different biases - over three hundred at the last count, and there are many different types of bias.

There are the obvious ones like bias against race, skin color, gender, body shape etc., but there are other types as well. Some of them are less obvious, for example, like a bias against people who chew gum or towards people who dress a certain way, or for or against someone with a certain accent or for or against men with ponytails. These tend to be easier to identify – in some cases, they are conscious and some cases, nonconscious. It does, however, take some explicit and conscious thought on behalf of each of us to recognize where we are biased.

Let's address one of the many elephants in the room. There is nothing subtle and nonconscious about someone who has elected to deliberately, frequently and publicly make racist comments, perform racist acts or become involved in groups that intend to discriminate against any specific group of people. We can divide these people into four groups:

> Those who are consciously racist and unwilling to change their minds.
> Those who are consciously racist, and whose minds might be open to change.
> Those who are nonconsciously racist and who, once it is pointed out, are eager to change.
> Those who are nonconsciously racist and who, once it is pointed out, are unwilling to change.
> Those who have, by accident, made a racist comment, and regret it the minute they do.

Clearly any remediation approach will be different for each category.

This chapter, however, will focus on nonconscious biases. As you will have seen in the section on Today's Reality, there are plenty of conscious, systemic and structural biases out there. Hopefully, this book will draw some of them into the open-air. But changing the minds of people who have consciously chosen to be biased, while of major importance, is not something that we can address here. Cultural mores, major institutional reforms and state and national laws will have greater effect. Our task is to focus on the biases that operate unknown within all of us and over which we may have some degree of influence and/or control.

Researchers have identified over three hundred biases. Not all of them have an impact on the topic of this book. We examined each of the three hundred and asked whether it would likely impact discrimination or racism. There's good news and bad news. The good news is that we were able to reduce it to only sixty biases! That's also the bad news. There are still sixty of them. And let's take this as the opportunity to restate something: these are not the obvious, directly observable, conscious biases of, for example, skin color, gender, sexual preference etc. The sixty are the ones that operate at a deeper level – and the fact that there are sixty of them that may have a nonconscious impact on our thinking, decision-making and actions when it comes to issues like discrimination and racism, illustrates the immensity of the problem that we face. For those readers that want to go into more detail, we have included a description of each of the sixty in Appendix B.

Before we begin digging deeper, a couple of words of explanation and caveats.

First, we are using the formal names for these biases that are used by the scientists that research these things. If you find it difficult to remember the formal names, then don't bother. Just focus on the meaning and potential impact of them.

Second, not all of them are called "biases" – some are called "syndromes" or "effects" or other things, but they are all used by the brain the same way as biases.

Third, they often interact with each other with some of them re-enforcing each other and some counteracting each other.

Fourth, not all of these biases apply in every situation, and we are not all subject to all of them. But most of us are subject to many of them.

To make it a little easier, we have identified six classes of biases.

Three of these classes are focused on us as individuals; the first one is the class of biases that come about when we are comparing ourselves, as individuals, with others. The second of these classes focuses on biases associated with the brain's reluctance to change. The final class regarding us as individuals is about biases concerned with how we are influenced in our thinking.

The final three classes, address biases that are concerned with how we behave in groups. The first of these is how we think of ourselves as a group. Then we look at biases about how we regard other groups, or other people that are not in our group. The final class looks at biases about how we justify our behavior.

In each class, we have identified what we believe to be the one or two most critical biases; we have then added the other biases which are associated with this class.

Class 1 Biases:	Comparing ourselves as individuals to others
Critical Bias	Actor-Observer Bias
Class 2 Biases:	Our reluctance to change as individuals
Critical Biases	Anchoring Effect Confirmation Bias
Class 3 Biases:	Things that influence our individual thinking
Critical Biases	Illusion of Truth Effect Ladder of Inference

Class 4 Biases:	How we view our group
Critical Biases	Bandwagon Effect Ingroup bias
Class 5 Biases:	How we view other groups
Critical Biases	Ultimate Attribution Error
Class 6 Biases:	How we justify what we do
Critical Biases	Framing Effect

Class 1 Biases: The Individual

This class of biases are associated with the process of comparing ourselves, as individuals, with other people. Many of these biases are oriented towards our own self-esteem; they provide a foundation for us to feel good about ourselves, and to feel superior to other people. We tend to believe that our actions are justified, that our opinions are grounded in fact, and that our decisions are not only fact based and rational but are fully thought through.

Actor-Observer Bias: We tend to explain other people's behavior by emphasizing their personality and de-emphasizing their situation. When we explain our own behavior, we let ourselves off the hook and tend to do the reverse. We blame our situation and de-emphasize our personality. *(You may hear this also as the Fundamental Attribution Error).*

The net effect of this is that we hold other people to different moral standards than we would hold ourselves even if we were in the same situation. In other words, we give ourselves an "out." We justify what <u>we</u> do as appropriate to the situation that we face, yet we blame <u>other people's</u> actions on their personalities. This contributes to racism by allowing our brains to attribute broad generalities about "race" to specific situations or attribute a set of characteristics to an entire class of people rather than looking at each of them as unique Individuals.

Here is one way it plays itself out in every-day life. If someone else is late we reach a rapid conclusion that the person is unreliable. If we are late, even if it is by the same amount, or with the same frequency, we will offer traffic as an excuse.

"Those people are just lazy. Why don't they just get a job."

"It's important to make the distinction between passing on required information, which is what I do and being a gossip, which is what he does."

> Take a moment and think about one of Jason's stories and reflect on how this class of bias impacted the thinking of one of the stakeholders involved in Jason's stories.

Class 2: Reluctance to Change

The class of biases that are associated with the brain's reluctance to change. In the earlier section, we talked about the brain's reluctance to change i.e. to even entertain the integration of data which conflicts with what we think we already know. This series of biases start to explain some of the reasons for this. In addition, our brain feels rewarded when we act consistently from one day to the next. It gives us a better sense of prediction. These biases contribute to racism by helping to preserve ingrained or established views, practices, or norms, even when they may no longer be true or if they have become outdated or if they were never true in the first place.

In many ways, the next two biases can be considered the "mothers-of-all-biases" in that they are both so widespread.

Anchoring Effect: This robust concept was introduced by two renowned psychologists Tversky & Kahneman in 1974 and has been the subject of many studies since. In essence it says that once an "anchor" has been introduced into our brains, that is the standard against which we make judgements and decisions, even though the anchor may have absolutely nothing to do with the thing we are making a decision about. We have a tendency to rely too heavily, or "anchor," on that one trait or piece of information when making subsequent decisions or choices (usually the first piece of information acquired on that subject). This anchoring effect is extremely widespread and arises in many instances where you would least expect it.

An 'anchor' in the brain can be placed in a number of ways, often by words, questions, numbers or graphics. The really sad and insidious aspects of this bias are that we often don't know it has been placed in our brains. The impact of anchoring has been measured in a broad array of different domains, such as price estimates, estimates of self-efficacy, probability assessments, legal judgments, negotiations and many others. Also, the impact of the anchoring influence can be drastic and unconnected with the subject at hand. In a famous experiment the price that someone was willing to pay for an item in an auction was influenced by the last two digits of their social security number!!!

In another series of experiments in wine and liquor stores, it was found that the music played influenced people's buying decisions. French music playing influenced people to buy more French wines.

On a more personal note, have you ever purchased something because it was 50% off but wouldn't have bought it if that mark-down hadn't caught your attention? That's anchoring at work.

> Take a moment and think about one of Jason's stories and reflect on how this class of bias impacted the thinking of one of the stakeholders involved.

Confirmation Bias: We have a tendency to search for, interpret, focus on, and remember information in a way that confirms our preconceptions. It doesn't matter what your background, religious or political leanings, without explicitly deciding to do otherwise, most of us tend to hang out in those spaces which confirm and support our beliefs. It's like a warm, cozy blanket. The brain doesn't have to think hard.

The impact? If you listen to CNN, then you will probably always listen to CNN; if you listen to Fox News, likewise.

In addition, the more confident we feel about our position or a belief that we hold, the more this bias is likely to show up.

Furthermore, as we listen to other people's positions and beliefs, our brains fail to make use of the strength of others' disconfirming opinions to alter our own but take those strengths into account when their opinions confirm our own. Research has been shown that, deep within our brains, there is reduced neural sensitivity to the strength of others' opinions when their opinions are disconfirming. Our existing judgments alter the neural representation of strength of this new information, leaving us less likely to alter opinions in the face of disagreement. If someone has predisposed attitudes toward a particular class of people, this bias will tempt them to only pay attention to information that supports that view and ignore anything that contradicts it.

> Take a moment and think about one of Jason's stories and reflect on how this class of bias impacted the thinking of one of the stakeholders involved.

Class 3: The way we are influenced

The class of biases that explain how we are influenced in our thinking. Our brains are influenced by many things. Some influences are general in that they seem to apply to many people across many cultures; these are such things as authority figures, other people's opinions, scarcity, and the need to return a favor. Others are more oriented towards our individual experiences and background.

Illusion of Truth Effect: People are more likely to identify as true, those statements that they have previously heard (even if they cannot consciously remember having heard them), regardless of the actual validity of the statement. In other words, a person is more likely to believe a familiar statement than an unfamiliar one. Even drastic untruths can enter our common knowledge base, by the use of repetition.

We would also hope that if we are forearmed with knowledge, then we won't be influenced by untruthful repetition. Unfortunately, it turns out that that is not the case. Inside the brain, repeated statements are easier to process, and subsequently perceived to be more truthful, than new statements, even if we have knowledge that support the new statements. [12]

The danger with untruthful or unvalidated statements being repeated, is that the listener tends only to hear the allegation, and not any of the caveats and qualifications that might follow the statements – like, this news has not been validated. This gets to be even more insidious if the news is being reported by a trustworthy, reputable news source as if it were fact.

And surely, if the statements themselves or the information contained therein, are implausible or preposterous, our brains will not be so influenced? Once again, this is not the case. We are still taken in. Fazio et all summarize it this way:

"Our results indicate that the illusory truth effect is highly robust and occurs across all levels of plausibility. Therefore, even highly implausible statements will become more plausible with enough repetition." [13]

Scary huh?

Ladder of Inference: This concept was introduced by Chris Argyris [14] in the early 1990's and demonstrates how we take a small piece of data and, mostly nonconsciously, make inferences about people, events and situations. Then we form opinions, make decisions and act in accordance with those inferences, which we believe to be totally true.

The steps of the ladder go like this:

1. *We observe a person's or group's behavior or statement*
2. *We focus on certain parts of the behavior; often that will depend on how the behavior is framed or how our attention is directed to focus*
3. *We summarize the behavior. Our brains don't like keeping all the detail – we just want the gist of what is going on*
4. *If we don't have all the data, or a complete picture, we fill in the gaps*
5. *We interpret that data through the lens of our biases, our own world view, and our previous experience, either with that person or similar people or group of people*
6. *We summarize, as we mentioned above, our brains are not good at keeping all of the detail hanging around*
7. *We make assumptions about that person and the narrative that we have told ourselves.*
8. *We draw conclusions or inferences about that person*
9. *We make decisions, engage in arguments and choose actions based upon those inferences*

This sequence happens very quickly and, mostly, nonconsciously. It gets worse, however. Once we have run up that ladder, our confirmation bias tends to ensure that, from then on, we seek out and only entertain data that confirm our conclusions and inferences. We often hear that accompanied by the phrase "See. I told you so."

One way to avoid this inference making, is to go back down the ladder, and identify <u>the actual data</u> that you personally observed (not hearsay) that caused these various internal leaps. What actually happened? What did that person actually say? What have you based your opinion on?

The insidious side of this part of human nature is that it plays on our natural inclination to fall into broad and simple explanations that appear to be true because they are so commonplace, even if they are false. A racist narrative will eventually be viewed as truth if it appears in the news enough times.

> Take a moment and think about one of Jason's stories and reflect on how this class of bias impacted the thinking of one of the stakeholders involved

Class 4: How we see our group

The class of biases that offer an explanation about how we see 'our group' and members of our group. Most of us like to be with people that we like and that are just like us. Our ingroup! It makes us feel comfortable and safe. We nonconsciously assign (positive) characteristics to our in-group and tend to contrast those characteristics with those who are not in our ingroup. We treat the people in our in-group differently to how we treat those who are not.

We form ingroups, often without knowing it, in a very short time. Whereas it used to be that ingroups were primarily geographically based, social media has made it easier to rapidly form ingroups across locations.

If the Anchoring effect and Confirmation bias are the mothers-of-all-biases, these next two biases have to be right up there with them in their ubiquity.

Bandwagon Effect: Our tendency to do (or believe) things because many other people do (or believe) the same. Related to groupthink and herd behavior. We are all influenced by what other people think. It is very difficult to hold beliefs that differ from one's own group – and even more difficult to express them in public.

The bandwagon effect has impact on everything between voting and buying luxury goods, and there is a vast amount of research on all aspects of the effect. Most of the research suggests that we are all susceptible to the opinions of other people; in the age of social media many web-sites have made effective use of this effect, FaceBook "likes" (in helping people form opinions) and Yelp (in making purchase choices or attendance selections) being two prime examples.

The research clearly shows a bandwagon effect in polling and subsequent voting choices; the resulting impact, however, is less than clear. On the one hand, the tendency for people to want to vote with the winner, will give an advantage to the leading candidate in a poll. On the other hand, the tendency for some people to want to vote for the underdog, will give the trailing candidate an advantage. In either case, however, people tend to be swayed by how other people will vote – or at least say how they intend to vote!

Where this effect gets to be worrisome is when it is combined with, for example, the Illusion of Truth Effect; we can become influenced by the stated beliefs of others, even though how they reached those beliefs may simply be based upon the repetition of untruths.

If someone is surrounded by racism, especially from people in their ingroup, it becomes easy to fall into those same attitudes.

> Take a moment and think about one of Jason's stories and reflect on how this class of bias impacted the thinking of one of the stakeholders involved

Ingroup bias: The tendency for people to give preferential treatment to others they perceive to be members of their own groups.

The APA [h] definition is as follows: [15]

> *"The tendency to favor one's own group, its members, its characteristics, and its products, particularly in reference to other groups. The favoring of the **ingroup** tends to be more pronounced than the rejection of the outgroup, but both tendencies become more pronounced during periods of intergroup contact."*

This bias has impact in a wide variety of situations, probably too numerous to address here. In relation to the subject of this book, it is easy to see that we need to understand the impact that ingroup bias has on racial and ethnic minorities in, at least, the following spaces: the public at large, on police treatment and the judicial process. For the sake of brevity, we are choosing to ignore the many other areas where ingroup bias shows up, for example, sports teams and violence, medical diagnosis and treatment of racial and ethnic minorities and the political impacts of racism and discrimination.

There are many impacts of ingroup bias, but, in summary, they are:

- *We are more likely to reward ingroup members for good behavior*
- *We are more likely to have heightened empathy toward ingroup members*

The opposite is also true. Less rewards and empathy for people in the outgroup.

---

[h] APA = American Psychological Association

These impacts are even stronger when the members of the ingroup have social ties in addition to simply being members of the group.

Ingroup bias seems to make sense from an evolutionary point of view; it would have provided an immediate way to have reduced uncertainty and hence increased survival possibilities. Another body of research in support of ingroup bias being evolutionary advantageous suggests that there is increased neural responses to perceived pain of same-race vs other race individuals.

In other words, our brains are wired to think differently about people of the same race, versus people of different races.

To be clear, all of us belong to a multitude of ingroups, and those ingroups can be formed very quickly, even within minutes. Gender, ethnicity, occupation, economic or social position, hobbies, pet ownership – have all become the basis for ingroups to form. There is nothing wrong with being in an ingroup, per se.

There are, however, a couple of downsides which may not be immediately obvious; first, an ingroup can feel exclusive to anyone looking at it from the outside – that is, to members of the outgroup. That exclusion can give a sense of rejection or disenfranchisement just by the fact of not being part of the ingroup. That is bad enough, but then the second downside comes into play. Members of an ingroup can feel and demonstrate a sense of superiority to members of the outgroup – and this is often the beginning of prejudice.

Take a moment and think about what must be going on in the brains of the people who are not in the ingroup. What level of threat state do you think they might be under? To what degree is their logical brain engaged on a daily basis?

Class 5: How we view other groups

This class covers those biases that explain how we view and think about those people that are not part of our group. Once we have formed an ingroup, the group tends to develop a set of "shared" opinions about people who are not part of the ingroup. The group tends to simplify the view it has of others and lump every individual member of the outgroup as having the same characteristics. In some cases, the members of the ingroup privately might disagree with the "shared" opinions of the group, but often will not speak up and won't rock the boat.

Ultimate Attribution Error: Thomas Pettigrew originated the term in 1979 [16] and explained it as follows: Ultimate attribution error occurs when ingroup members (1) attribute negative outgroup behavior to internal factors (more than they would for identical ingroup behavior), and (2) attribute positive outgroup behavior to one or more of the following causes: (a) a fluke or exceptional case, (b) luck or special advantage, (c) high motivation and effort, and (d) external situational factors.

This is where we really start to get into trouble.

> *"This attributional double standard makes it virtually impossible for outgroup members to break free of prejudice against them, because their positive actions are explained away while their failures and shortcomings are used against them."* [17]

Let's look at three studies illustrating this bias:

One study found that white students were more likely to interpret a shove as violent -- and more likely to explain it in the form of blame -- when the shove came from a black person than a white person.

Another study found that Hindu participants were more likely to make dispositional attributions for negative behaviors than positive behaviors when the actor was Muslim but showed the opposite pattern when the actor was Hindu.

And a review of 58 different experiments found that on traditionally masculine tasks, male successes were more likely than female successes to be attributed to ability, whereas male failures were more likely than female failures to be attributed to bad luck or lack of effort.

In other words, we give our ingroup a break and we don't give a break to the outgroup!

Take a moment and think about one of Jason's stories and reflect on how this class of bias impacted the thinking of one of the stakeholders involved

Class 6: Some ways we justify our actions

The class of biases that looks at biases regarding how we justify our behavior. The brain is really good at making stuff up. We take our nonconscious decisions, choices and actions and use the rational part of our brain to come up with a plausible narrative. We develop explanations for our actions, often simply to justify them to other ingroup members.

Framing Effect: A bias whereby we draw different, and possibly opposite, conclusions from the same information, depending on how that information is presented and anchored.

Digging slightly deeper, it is when we are faced with two choices that are "logically equivalent" but, at first glance, do not appear to be the same. Typically, each choice highlights either a positive or a negative attribute relating to the choice.

Let's look at a couple of examples:

"This policy would result in 10% unemployment" vs "This policy we will ensure 90% employment."

"The Covid-19 pandemic is likely to mean that 2% of those infected will die" vs "The good news is that 98% of people are likely to survive Covid-19."
Druckman [18] explains it to us nicely:

> "Specifically, a framing effect is said to occur when, in the course of describing an issue or event, a speaker's emphasis on a subset of potentially relevant considerations causes individuals to focus on these considerations when constructing their opinions."

The Framing Effect is so powerful, that it is deliberately and frequently used in Advertising and Politics. Indeed, it is so powerful in politics that some countries ban political advertising in the final days before an election.

> Take a moment and think about one of Jason's stories and reflect on how this class of bias impacted the thinking of one of the stakeholders involved

Let's make some final comments on biases. First a reminder. There's nothing wrong with biases. The brain needs them in order to function efficiently. It is when one or more biases impact us or someone else negatively and that we are unaware of the impact … that's when we can get into trouble.

Compounding the issue is that biases rarely show up singly. They join together to form a roving band making snap decisions in the recesses of our brains.

Let's take a look at a couple of examples. The first is based upon some actual research and is reported in a paper written by Kathleen Nalty and published in The Colorado Layer in 2016; she references some work to investigate whether attorneys exhibit bias. [19] Specifically they were looking for " … whether attorneys believe African Americans produce inferior written work and that Caucasians are better writers."

The researchers developed a memo that contained 22 errors (spelling, grammar, technical writing, factual and analytical). 60 partners in attorney firms were told that the memo was written by a third-year associate named Thomas Meyer. Half of the partners were told that Meyer was Caucasian, and half were told that he was African American. Here are the results:

	Caucasian Meyer	African American Meyer
Overall rating	4.1	3.2
Spelling Errors	2.9	5.8

In addition, the attorneys found more technical and factual errors and made more critical comments with respect to the African American Meyer. In addition, the researchers found that "… the female and racially/ethnically diverse partners were just as likely as white male partners to be more rigorous …" in their examination of the memo written by the African American Meyer.

We can imagine that there are multiple biases at work here – at the very least, anchoring, confirmation bias, ingroup bias, and attribution biases in various forms.

Tom has a story of an African American man who was the factory manager at a global consumer goods manufacturer. Since he spent most of his time in the factory, like all of his employees, he wore a factory jumpsuit. He was a member of the Executive team and on a regular basis, walked across the road to attend the Executive team meeting. After some time, he realized that nobody took into account any of his comments or suggestions. So, one day he took a different tack. He changed into a business suit, with shirt and tie. All of a sudden, he was listened to.

Once again, we can speculate what biases were in operation here. But the experience shows that "racism" or prejudice is not limited to just skin color. It can apply to literally any grouping of people, under the right circumstances.

Habits. To the brain, habits have a benefit similar to biases. It means the brain doesn't have to consciously think about everything all of the time. A habit is a set of responses laid down in the past. Remember that the brain is constantly looking for a way to be efficient with information. Habits create that efficiency even in cases where it may not always be the best choice.

Let's look at a social habit by way of example. A good friend of yours comes to you with a tough problem asking for your help in resolving it. You might respond in a number of ways. On the one hand, you might spend some time asking questions and coaching the person and help them think through different possible solutions. On the other hand, you might simply give them your opinion as to how to solve it. Research indicates that without explicit training, we tend to default one way or other, with many people defaulting to the directive approach. We do this for a number of reasons; we love being sought out for our opinion or it seems to be the quickest way to resolve the issue – and be able to get back to what we were doing! There's no right or wrong way to respond – but we all tend to default one way or the other. Out of habit.

What about when request for help comes to you from outside your normal community of interest – your ingroup? Do you respond the same way? Or do you default to a different habit?

The fact of having habits is neither good nor bad. They are efficient, and we don't have to spend conscious brain energy thinking about them. We tend to make judgments about habits – our own and other peoples' – as "good" habits or "bad" habits. Overall, unless we make special efforts, they are frequently out of our awareness, are unintentional, and are often uncontrollable.

The reasons that you will want to identify habits is the same as for biases, i.e.,

- ➢ to make sure that you are consciously aware of them
- ➢ to make a decision as to whether they are still useful to you at this stage of your life
- ➢ to make sure that they are appropriate in this day and age

One approach to identifying habits is some self-reflection. For some people, this is simply a matter of taking some time to look inward and is an easy activity; if you can reflect and identify your own habits, that is excellent.

Another step might be to pay attention the next time you notice yourself getting an emotion at work or home, e.g., angry, tense, stressed, on the one hand, or feeling light, happy, and content on the other. Ask yourself questions like, what am I thinking? What expectations do I have? When have I noticed this before? Who is around? What just happened? What did I interpret from that? If you like to keep a journal, then jot some notes down; if not, then just notice.
Then ask yourself the following questions: What is the impact of my habit? What is the impact on me? What is the impact when I am working with another person? What is the impact to the group of people with whom I work?

In a little more detail, Charles Duhigg, [20] an eminent researcher on habits, suggests that there are three parts to a habit, namely a trigger, a routine, and a reward. As you look at your own habits, you could look at what triggers you, what the routine is, and what the reward is.

Let's look at a simple personal example, brushing your teeth. What is the trigger? For most of us, it is the act of waking up. We do it automatically either just when we have woken or after breakfast or both. The routine? We tend to do it at the same time, in the same place, in the same posture, and, for most people, in the same sequence every day. This may be the reason why I have had so much difficulty in adopting the use of an electric toothbrush. It requires me to do something different. It is not the same habit. Now, how about the reward? Two-fold. Socially acceptable breath (short-term) and healthier teeth (long-term).

A good start in the investigation of our own habits is to name as many of them as you can (good and bad) and outline the impact they have on you and on others. If you get stuck, ask people who know you well. For each habit you identify, you could then look at the triggers, the routine, and the reward.

Jason tells a story about how when he first enters a room and is confronted by a group of men, most often middle-aged white men, he defaults to a habit – introduce the topic of sports. Most of the time it works well, and he is accepted as part of the group. Occasionally, it backfires. Here's Jason:

"I have this habit. I hate when people feel awkward around me, and I guess I assume that most white people, upon meeting me for the first time, may feel this way so I will quickly fill in the conversational gap not only to make them feel less awkward but also as a means of protecting myself. I hate feeling like an oddity or someone to avoid, so I go out of my way to make all people feel comfortable. For example, if I'm meeting with a group of middle age white men then I may defer to a conversation around sports, because who doesn't like to talk about sports? While this usually works, it is not a sure proof method of connecting. In 2019 I was meeting with my client's Board of Directors. I remember having a conversation about sports with a group of men and the conversation turned to "Why are all the good athletes black?" Sensing that this was going to go down a rabbit hole I attempted to pivot to a conversation about business. No dice. They didn't take my bait. I was sitting there listening to these men discuss the "physical superiority" of black athletes while praising the intelligence of quarterbacks such as John Elway, Peyton Manning and Tom Brady. All of this was code for, "blacks may be physically superior, but whites are far more intelligent." [i] At this point, I said, "Look, there are plenty of smart, physically capable black athletes. Besides, not all of us are bigger and stronger than athletes of other races." And that is the moment that I realized "You done messed up, Son" as my father used to say to me when I exercised my superhuman ability to put my foot squarely in my mouth. I was sitting there making the case that not all

---

[i] To take the sports discussion slightly further, this is a great example of both confirmation bias and ultimate attribution bias in action. They completely ignored other great black QBs like Russell Wilson, Lamar Jackson (reigning MVP), Patrick Mahomes (Super Bowl winner – black father white mother), Warren Moon, Duante Culpepper, etc. They have also ignored the terrible QBs over the years that were white … Johnny Manziel, Ryan Leaf, Harrington, Josh Rosen, etc.

black people are physically superior to other races and yet I failed to grasp the fact that I am physically towering over these men. They probably stood between 5'7 and 5'9, and may have weighed on average around 170 lbs. One of the men looked up at me and asked, "Jason, how tall are you?" I answered, "6'3". This was followed by, "How much do you weigh?" I answered, "270lbs." How broad are your shoulders?" I said, "48 inches across" and he looks at his co-conspirators and said, "You look like an NFL Linebacker! You are the biggest person in this room. I rest my case." This, of course, was followed by laughter from his colleagues and an appreciative (demeaning?) slap on my shoulder as if to say, "C'mon pal! You have to see the humor in this." I gave the man a polite smile and a slap on his shoulder (I could tell it hurt because he turned red) and said, "It's all fun and games, right?" At this point the meeting was called to order so I assumed my seat along the far wall, playing the "tolerant Negro" role while fuming inside. Eventually it was my turn to present and all I kept thinking was, "You better show these people exactly why you deserve to be in this room." I felt this intense pressure to be the best, despite the fact that I was the only subject matter expert on the particular issue I was brought in to discuss with the Board. Herein lies the challenge for people of color...we believe we have to be better and work twice as hard as white people because our respective races will be judged by the majority's interaction with us. In that moment, whether it be the boardroom or a casual interaction on a street corner, we become the sole caretaker for everything white America will believe about people who look like us.

So, I stood up and felt it coming...the nervous beads of sweat manifesting on my forehead. It is at this point that I asked if we could take a quick bathroom break because I had to make a couple of tweaks to the presentation based on "new information". I purposely went to a separate bathroom, away from everyone else. I stared at myself in the mirror, doused my face with water and repeated my mantra – "You deserve this" over and over again. You may be asking, "Why were you nervous, Jason?" Well, the simple answer is because I could not get the laughter of the men I spoke to prior to the meeting out of my head. It triggered me...it brought me back to the feeling of being an outsider my entire life. I hated the fact that I was bigger than the average person. I hated the fact that my skin tone would never allow me to pass for normal, unless I lived in the fictional afro-futuristic utopia of Wakanda!!! I hated feeling like my degrees, credentials and financial success all seemed to evaporate every time I was locked within the psychological battlefield called "navigating white spaces." So, in that moment, I locked in. I knew I belonged, but more importantly I was going to make them tell me I belonged. I went into the board room with the idea that I was going to eat everyone's lunch. I was going to be the best that they had ever seen. Forty-five minutes later, the very men that laughed at my expense prior to the meeting were the same ones coming up to me telling me how wonderful my presentation was. I smiled with them, took in their compliments but I never dropped my guard because they had the power to hurt me and I would never allow them the opportunity to do so again. My best has to be so good that one day they decide to give someone who looks like me a chance. My best has to be better than what they believe. I get this and I accept it, but I will never get used to the sheer exhaustion associated with always being cognizant of never making a mistake, simply because I do not have the luxury of not being the best. Too many people, both real and imagined, depend on my getting it right."

> What do you see as some common habits that might impact the topic of this book – i.e. discrimination and racism?

If you are having any trouble answering the question in the box, here's a couple of situations to nudge your thoughts:

➢ If you are walking down the street and you look ahead and see that there is an African American woman walking towards you, what do you do? Cross the street or stay on the side you are on?

➢ If you are walking down the street and you look ahead and see that there is an African American man walking towards you, what do you do? Cross the street or stay on the side you are on?

➢ If you are checking out of a supermarket and there is choice of lanes, which lane do you choose, and why (assuming that they all have the same line length)

➢ If someone is driving slowly or erratically in front of you, when you finally pass them, what do you do? Look back at who was driving and make a conclusion about the person … and their group?

> Take a moment and think about one of Jason's stories and reflect on how habits may have impacted the thinking of one of the stakeholders involved.

c) Your Brain on Change

It's not surprising that most humans have a tough time in changing; our brains build and maintain mental models of everything – literally everything; and our brains like it when everything new that we learn aligns with that model. In addition, as you will just have read, there are a whole set of biases that we have that love to maintain the status quo. So, if the thought of changing some paradigms or preconceived notions is somewhat scary, you are not alone.

Yet, if we are going to move the issue of racism forward, then we are going to have to change a lot of brains! So, it might help us if we can learn how people change, how we can assist in their process, which people are not likely to change and why they don't, what we can do that works , and what we should not do.

The first thing for us to address is that, from a brain and behavioral perspective, not all of us approach change in the same way. As a result of all of our experiences, worldviews, biases, habits, personality traits and many other factors, we all react in different ways whenever we approach anything. For some people, learning something new, one aspect of change, can be a terrifying experience. For others, being given advice or feedback, feels like being told what to do – and they reject the information. So, if you are working on yourself, or working with someone else, recognize that we are <u>all</u> different. What will help one individual change, won't necessarily help the next person. We all have a bias to think that other people think the way that we do – and that can lead us into dangerous territory; just because a certain approach worked for us, the same approach may not work for someone else.

There are many explanations, models and approaches about how and why people do actually change. In order to provide a number of ways to approach change we will take a quick look at six of these explanations.

- ➤ Readiness to change
- ➤ Learning to change
- ➤ Influences
- ➤ Adoption of new ideas
- ➤ Resistance to change
- ➤ Conditions required for change to occur

Readiness. One of the places we might start is to recognize the old adage "ready, willing and able." These three factors are important in the world of change. Let's look at the first of these, readiness. Whether you, somebody else, or a group of people, is/are ready to change is important to know, as the approach you take will be different depending on where they are in their thinking.

James Prochaska [21] has spent a good deal of his career in studying change. While the focus of his studies has generally been about things like smoking cessation, his theories have been applied to many change processes, [i] so we think his approach is worth considering and may be relevant to changing people's minds when it comes to racism and discrimination.

He identified some assumptions and five stages for change as follows:

Assumptions:

- change takes time
- there are common tasks in each stage
- by tailoring an approach to match the stage of change the person is in, you will be more successful in helping that person to make lasting change.

Five official stages and one unofficial stage:

1. Precontemplation stage - the "ignorance is bliss" stage. People in this stage don't see a problem and consequently are not interested in changing their behavior.
2. Contemplation. People in this stage are "on the fence:" they acknowledge a problem but are not sure if the benefits of change outweigh the benefits of staying the same.
3. The third stage is Preparation. People in this stage see a problem and "testing the waters;" they take small steps towards change.
4. The fourth stage is Action. People in this stage have identified a plan for changing their behavior and have started to implement it.
5. The fifth stage is Maintenance. People in this stage have been engaging in the new behavior for at least six months.
6. The unofficial sixth stage is Relapse. People in this stage have, for whatever reason, "fallen off the wagon" and are engaging in the old behaviors.

---

[i] We think it a reasonable approach – his approach has been adapted to smoking cessation, exercise, low fat diet, radon testing, alcohol abuse, weight control, condom use for HIV protection, organizational change, use of sunscreens to prevent skin cancer, drug abuse, medical compliance, mammography screening, and stress management.

There is a more detailed description of this change readiness model in Appendix C.

If a person or a group in question, is in the first of these stages, it might be difficult to embark on a change. At the very least, it will require a different approach to the change and any support required. If the person or group in question is in the second stage, then consider very carefully whether this is the right time to invest that amount of effort and energy, and whether they are likely to be willing to incur the losses and personal cost involved. In both of these stages, the approach might be more about education and exposure, rather than a serious change effort.

If the person or group in question, is in stages three or four, then you are well on the way to supporting their change.

How can you tell where the person or group is? The simplest way is to get a general sense by raising the topics and introducing a discussion. A slightly more formal way is to ask some specific questions as shown in Appendix C. If you want to be even more formal you can find questionnaires via Google or Google Scholar.

Other researchers have expanded Prochaska's work. In the preparation phase and in the action phase, we often see an "Experimentation" component, that is the individual or group is trying out different ways of attempting the change. Seeing what works best. This experimentation is to be encouraged.

Once you have determined where the person or group in question is on the readiness scale, then you can start to design the change support approach that you might use. Once again, a reminder - there is no "one-size fits all approach" to any change process, let alone one as sensitive and emotion-filled as the one we are working on. The approaches that we suggest below regarding change are for you to consider as you put your own approach together.

Learning to Change. Dan Millman, a one-time Olympic gymnast and an instructor for trampoline, offers a "learning to change" model [22]; he noticed a multi-step learning process that his students typically went through, which he called the Ladder of Learning. We are going to adapt and leverage that model in thinking about how people might change with respect to racism.

> *1. The bottom rung of the ladder is where the individual in question is unable to recognize a racist thought, comment or action, even when it is deliberately illustrated by an expert in the field.*

2. The first step is when he/she is able to recognize it by an expert when it is being deliberately illustrated. They see why it might be offensive

3. The next step is that they are able to recognize it in past behaviors – either by themselves, or, more frequently, by other people.

4. Step four is when the individual in question is able to recognize it in him or herself – but after the event. At a later point in time, they catch themselves thinking about what they thought, said or did – and realize that there might have been a better way. This is a major breakthrough!

5. Then the individual in question is able to recognize it in him or herself – but immediately after the event. He/she should be congratulated.

6. The next step is for the individual in question to be able to recognize it in him or herself as it is happening – and, maybe, if he/she catches it in time, correct it.

7. Then the individual in question is able to prevent it from happening, but with conscious effort.

8. The final step is for the behavior to become nonconscious.

We include a picture of a ladder below for those of you who are more visual and hate lists!

Be careful. In some ways the picture of a ladder, with equal steps, is misleading. It is a relatively quick and easy step to go from the bottom of the ladder on to the first step. And the path to the third and fourth rung is fairly easy too. Then the going gets a little tougher. The step to the fifth rung happens fairly soon. But many people find the jump to the sixth rung more difficult. Seven gets more difficult and taking it to a nonconscious habit can take much longer.

8. It has become nonconscious behavior

7. Able to consciously prevent it from happening

6. Able to recognize in self – as it was happening and correct it consciously

5. Able to recognize in self – immediately after the event

4. Able to recognize in self – long after the event

3. Able to recognize in other students

2. Able to recognize in a professional

1. Unable to recognize in a professional

So, what makes it easier or more difficult to move up one step? In other words, once we understand the ladder, what influences our progress, and how do we know where we are now?

Influences. Cialdini [23] has identified six general principles of things that influence us. The six are Reciprocation, Social Proof, Commitment and Consistency, Liking, Authority, and Scarcity:

1. Reciprocation

Reciprocation recognizes that people feel indebted to those who do something for them or give them a gift; this is true even if the gift they are given is not something that they asked for or even voiced a want for. This happens at a nonconscious level. So, why is this influence important in our look at racism? For two reasons; first, is that it happens at a nonconscious level – if someone gives us a gift, we feel obliged to give them something back. So, beware of those bearing gifts. Second, is that if you want to influence someone, give them something first.

2. Social Proof

When people are uncertain about a course of action, they tend to look to those around them to guide their decisions and actions. They especially want to know what everyone else is doing – especially their peers. If peers are acting in a truly inclusive way, that can promote inclusiveness in others. However, the converse is also true. Behavior that excludes or denigrates a group is also contagious.

3. Commitment and Consistency

People do not like to back out of deals. We're more likely to do something after we've agreed to it verbally or in writing. People strive for consistency in their commitments. They also prefer to follow pre-existing attitudes, values, and actions. Once again this is important in a couple of ways. Commitments to overcome biases may help influence success in doing so, especially public commitments; secondly, making a small commitment is likely to lead to a larger commitment to the same thing. Our brains strive for consistency.

4. Liking

It has long been an adage in the sales field that, all other things being equal, people will do business with people they like. People prefer to say "yes" to those they know and like and are more likely to favor those who are physically attractive, similar to themselves, or who give them compliments. We are influenced in our choices by the things that we like or are attracted to or things that we don't like or are put off by. The converse of this is that if we only associate with people like ourselves, and that we like, then those who are different will be at an inherent disadvantage.

5. Authority

People respect authority. They want to follow the lead of real experts. Business titles, impressive clothing, and even driving an expensive, high-performing automobile are proven factors in lending credibility to any individual. Therefore, if leaders display racist or exclusionary attitudes or actions, even ones that are not intentional, then others may view those behaviors as acceptable. The converse is also true. True equality starts with strong leadership.

6. Scarcity

Basically, the less there is of something, the more valuable it is. The more rare and uncommon a thing, the more people want it. A relatively recent and somewhat familiar example is urban campers waiting overnight to pounce on the latest iPhone. If resources are in short supply, we might enter a threat state, and will be more likely to assume that others (especially those who are different) represent a threat to us having or achieving that scarce resource.

So, moving up the learning ladder requires an understanding of influence, including some of the concepts discussed by Cialdini, as described above. But it is not enough. It also requires, for many of us, fully adopting and embracing ideas that are new and different versus what we were taught, or what we might believe is true. Next, let's look at what influences whether or not our brains are open to, and able to accept, these new ideas.

Adoption of new ideas: In 1991 Geoffrey Moore wrote a seminal book called Crossing the Chasm; [24] it was about how people adopt technology. The subtitle is Marketing and Selling Technology Products to Mainstream Customers. Since then, his approach has been applied to many different areas. Three principles, in particular, from his book apply to the topic of racism and change. First, different people adopt new ideas at different rates – he gives three adoption categories. Second, people in each category adopt ideas for different reasons. Third, the majority of people, when considering the adoption of a new idea, want to reference people who are in the same category.

The adoption categories and their reasons for adoption are:

Category	Reasons to adopt something new
Pioneers:	To achieve a dream; have excitement or be different. They want to be on the leading edge and OK if it doesn't go perfectly smoothly.
Early adopters	To achieve a project or result that can be done easier with the new idea or product or approach, and they too will put up with it not working perfectly.
Early majority	To be safe. They want to see the product or approach being used by a number of their peers. The approach needs to be comprehensive and free of faults.
Late majority	To be ultra-safe. They want many testimonials. They want to have their own team be convinced it is the right choice.
Laggards	May never use the new product, service or take a new approach.

The grayed bar between the first two categories above and the last three is deliberate. The last three are much harder to convince and require a very different, more thoughtful approach.

Resistance to Change – Part 1. Influencing those who are in the Early Majority, Late Majority, or Laggard categories above, will require a more structured and deliberate approach to driving change and overcoming biases. We have all experienced this; whenever we listen to people talk about change, the conversation invariably turns to people's resistance to change. From the brain's perspective, we know why that is. The models that our brains hold and our brain's reluctance to integrate conflicting data into those models. But what about other reasons?

One model that provides a useful basis for discussion is a structure known as Gleicher's Formula. [25]

The latest version of this formula identifies four factors that must be present for <u>any</u> change to actually occur. These are:

A Compelling **<u>Vision</u>** (V) multiplied by

a set of clearly defined **<u>First Steps</u>** (F) multiplied by

<u>believability</u> (B) multiplied by

<u>dissatisfaction</u> with the Status Quo (D)

and they must be significantly greater than the

<u>Personal Cost of Change</u> (R)

For the mathematically minded, the formula is represented by the following equation:

$$V \times F \times B \times D \gg R$$

<u>Vision</u> It is easier for our brains to imagine change if we have a picture or vision of what we are aiming at. If it is possible for this to be an actual visual image, [k] so much the better, but in many cases, a verbal or written description will suffice. So, if we are going to help people move toward a more diverse, equitable and inclusive society, we need to provide a description of what that looks and feels like, and how it will include the person listening to our description. The more evocative and emotional that description, the better.

<u>First Steps</u> This component is often reflected in the question: "I am interested, engaged, but don't know what to do." We don't have to give the full plan on how to get to achieving the vision, but we have to provide some steps to start on the journey. For some people, these need to be very concrete steps. For others, it can be just some pointers in the right direction.

<u>Believability:</u> The vision and first steps must be believable. They cannot be pie in the sky; the vision can be a stretch, but it must be realistic and achievable given the current context. If it's too far out ahead of the imagination of the average person, then the

---

[k] A significant portion of the brain's neural circuitry is devoted to visual processing.

change will get dismissed as too difficult. And this believability needs to be both at the emotional and logical level.

Dissatisfaction: If people are happy with what is going on in the current context, or are unaware with what is going on, they will not be dissatisfied – and change will not occur. It is very clear that certain slices of today's world are not dissatisfied with what is going on in the way of racism. This will require some education.

Personal Cost of Change: This may have many attributes including overcoming the fear of change, losses involved, the amount of time, feeling out of one's depth, feeling like stepping into the unknown, money involved, psychological issues, emotional issues, social attributes – and many more. It is highly individual and needs to be dealt with as such – and cannot be glossed over if we are going to get real change to occur.

Sorry to bring this up now, but we are going to have to tread gently into the field of algebra; we suspect that is not, to say the least, everyone's favorite topic. But hang on in there. It is, in fact, pretty easy. The above change formula is expressed as an algebraic equation; this implies that, under the laws of algebra, if one or more of the factors on the left-hand side of the equation is less than "1" then the result will become very small and is unlikely, therefore, to overcome resistance to the change or personal cost. Clearly, according to this formula, if any of the factors is zero, or non-existent, then no change is likely to occur! This is a key point.

So, what does this mean for individual and group change? It means that if you are about to embark on a change, we need to be able to say a wholehearted "yes" to each of the four items identified above – at an individual and a group level. Yes, he/she/they have a clear picture of the future state. Yes, he/she/they know some clear options of what they can do first. He/she/they believe that the future state is realistic and achievable all of the above. Finally, he/she/they are dissatisfied with what is going on today.

It also means that we need to address the personal cost of change – and give people an opportunity to both voice [1] their concerns and know that they were heard.

_____

[1] For some people, of the most serious threats to their brain is if they feel that their voice is not heard.

> What might a vision of a truly egalitarian, diverse and equitable enterprise, community or society be? The richer the description, the better.
>
> What are the first steps that you might take? What are the first steps that your enterprise could take? What are the first steps that your community might take?
>
> How might you increase the believability that the vision is achievable?
>
> What could you do to increase people's dissatisfaction with the status quo?
>
> What could you do alleviate the fear that the cost of change is going to be high?

Resistance to Change – Part 2. Being told what to do. In many of his lectures, Phil will ask the audience the following question: "How many of you like to be told what to do? Please raise your hand." Inevitably, initially no one raises their hand. After a minute or so, one brave soul will timidly raise their hand and make the following statement: "I do, sometimes." When asked about those occasions, it always comes down to "When I don't know what to do" or "When the stakes are really high."

In general, we hate to be told what to do. When someone tells us we should do something, or that we need to change, not only do we resist as we describe above in Part 1, but we resist the very process of being told what to do! This is true even if we are not being told what t do, but the <u>perception</u> to our brain is that we are. If you think back to the section in bias on the "righting reflex" any sense of an attempt to convince or persuade, can feel like being told what to do. And we reject it. In many cases, the person doing the telling is simply trying to "help" – but it doesn't feel like that to the brain of the recipient.

Miller and Rollnick [26] describe the reactions to being told what to do, as follows:

> *Angry (agitated, annoyed, irritated, not heard, not understood)*
> *Defensive (discounted, judged, justifying, oppositional, unwilling to change)*
> *Uncomfortable (ashamed, overwhelmed, eager to leave)*
> *Powerless (passive, one-down, discouraged, disengaged)*
>
> *"In fact, sometimes in this interaction, the person being "helped" concludes that he or she doesn't want to make the change."*

The bottom line, is that if it feels like being told what to do, not only may we resist the content of the change, but we will rebel against the process.

Conditions for change to occur. There is a greater chance of change to occur, if the recipient feels [27]:

Engaged (interested, cooperative, liking the deliverer of the message, ready to keep talking)
Empowered (able to change, hopeful, optimistic)
Open (accepted, comfortable, safe, respected)
Understood (connected, heard, listened to)

In addition, our research shows that the deliverer of the message needs to be trusted and credible.

We need to create all of these conditions if we are going to increase the chance of the message being heard.

Consistency. The brain likes consistency. Consistency is the opposite of change and so provides the brain with a sense of safety and comfort. We can use this dynamic as part of a change support process. If, instead of asking people to make major changes, we ask them to make small, easily acceptable and easily adoptable changes. Once a small change has been adopted, research shows that the brain is more likely to adopt a larger change – the decision has already been taken to adopt the small change, and the desire for consistency drives the brain to accept the larger change. In addition, we know that on the ways to gain success for larger change, is to break it into much smaller steps.

Friends. For some people, change is relatively easy. For others, it is really hard. One of the reasons it is hard, is that none of us lives our lives in isolation [m] – the 'system' that surrounds us, expects us to behave in the same way that we always have. If we change, then it puts a shock into our surrounding system – and, very often, the system will push back. Our friends and family become disturbed when we, apparently to them, all of a sudden, change our minds on a belief that we have held for a long time.

This extra resistance by the system of friends and family can be avoided in a couple of ways, neither of which is particularly easy. The first is to avoid the people (friends and family) that are likely to resist your change; at least avoid them until such time as you become comfortable in your own changed mind. The second is to let them know what you are planning to do and ask them to help you – and always give a reason why you

---

[m] Well, at least not until the COVID-19 pandemic in 2020

are going to go ahead with the change. There's a lot of research that suggests that people are much more willing to support an action, if there is a reason attached to it. (By the way, it also turns out that the reason doesn't have to be particularly valid or one that they agree with – they just need to hear something that is a reason.) Most people, when asked to help, even if they don't agree with your direction, might be willing to do something. And be prepared when they ask, "And what help do you need?" The help might be something as simple as "Please just listen and don't give me advice." The third, which is getting into the more difficult domain, might be to ask them to come along with you on the change journey. Some people are willing to jump on to your bandwagon, if you present your ideas firmly enough. Finally, if none of these approaches is going to work with your friends and family, decide whether the personal cost of change is too great; at least too great at this time.

d) Other influences

This section adds some other dimensions or explanations about some important aspects of how our brains work. They are not presented in anything other than alphabetical sequence.

Alcohol: The effects of alcohol on the brain are well known; this is true both in the world of brain research and in the general population. When we drink there are a number of things that happen, in addition to thinking that we can sing Bohemian Rhapsody better than Freddie Mercury! One of the areas of the brain that suffers when we consume alcohol, is the rational part of the brain that we discussed in Chapter 2. As a reminder, it is the part of the brain that provides, amongst other things, logic, rationality, self-control, empathy, and risk assessment. Alcohol diminishes the ability of the rational part of the brain to exhibit these functions.

So, what's this got to do with racism? When we drink alcohol, the self-control functions of the rational brain are highly impacted. We are less likely to be able to control the biases and habits that are wired into the emotional part of the brain. The filter in the rational brain that we typically employ is significantly diminished. This effect was well-illustrated recently by a man that had drunk six or seven beers and proceeded to berate one of the wait-staff when he refused to wear a mask. He proceeded to hurl racial (and other) slurs in her direction.

The following morning, when shown a video of how he had behaved, he was ashamed and denied the fact that he was a racist. He put it down to the physical impact of alcohol.

An additional problem is that a major part of the rational brain is not fully formed until well into the twenties and is more susceptible to the impact of alcohol.

Allyship: While not strictly an influence, the concept of becoming an ally is profound, and hence we include it here. There are many suggestions to be found if you do a Google search on becoming an ally. One of the most approachable lists comes from Stephanie Creary in a recent HBR article [28] where she describes the LEAP model: [n]

> **L:** Listen and learn from your black colleagues' experiences.
> **E:** Engage with black colleagues in racially diverse and more casual settings.
> **A:** Ask black employees about their work and their goals.
> **P:** Provide your black colleagues with opportunities, suggestions, encouragement, and general support.

Categories: [29] In our minds, we nonconsciously divide people into categories for several reasons:
- We can discern differences
- There are differences in the size of different groups
- The categories are implicitly and explicitly used
- We assume that there are meaningful differences between groups
- They are labeled
- The labeling is perpetuated by most governmental organizations (e.g. census taking)

So why is this an issue? Roberts and Rizzo [30] again:

"Category labels can promote the belief that category members share an "essence" that grants them their identity."

---

[n] This approach can be applied to any group difference we are aware of.

In other words, once we give someone a label and identify some characteristic of that person, we assume that others in the same category have the same characteristic. It becomes even more pernicious, however:

> *"Category labels … additionally promote a descriptive-to-predictive tendency (i.e. believing that how a group is reflects how group members should be,) which supports racial stereotyping and prejudice."*

Note that this "predictive" effect tends to become exacerbated by our tendency to think of other categories than our own as "outgroups" and apply the ultimate attribution error of assuming that everyone in the other category is the same.

Community: The community that surrounds any given enterprise can have an effect on the ability of the enterprise to implement an inclusive culture. Research done by Humbert et al [31] shows that:

> *" … organizations cannot merely focus internally on building an inclusive culture; they must also consider how the community responds to diversity, particularly, when those responses are not aligned with the organization's vision for inclusion."*

Therefore, overcoming racism in a sub-set of a community, for example an enterprise, an individual church, or a school among a community where racism is highly prevalent will be difficult. Overcoming it for a person who lives in a more open and accepting community will be easier. Momentum within a community is critical. Whether a community is overcoming racism, or preserving it, the process will be contagious.

Courage: [o] Moving forward and addressing the issues of racism and discrimination will require many acts of courage. We thought it useful, therefore, to explain a little about courage. Courage, in its various forms, has been studied for several thousand years, perhaps even longer, and ranges from obvious physical courage to moral courage with many different types in between.

> *"Courage is viewed as the most universally admired virtue because it is grounded in self-sacrifice, serves the needs of others, and is needed to enact all of the other virtues."* [32]

---

[o] For a more detailed description on increasing courage, see Appendix E.

All aspects of courage, however, seem to have some common factors:

> The need to confront something, typically the status quo
> Embrace a change
> Face resistance
> Oppose a popular, but unhealthy idea
> Speak the truth
> Hear someone else's truth
> Pursue a lofty, and often, audacious goal
> Act intentionally
> Assess and acknowledge the risk involved
> Persist, in spite of fear
> Protect those in need

In the process of acting courageously, there are four stages

- *the tension that precedes action*
- *the choice to behave courageously*
- *the act itself*
- *the reflection that follows the act*

It is reasonable to assume that most, if not all, of these aspects are engaging one or more parts of the rational brain. "Assessment", "mindful action", "reasonable risk", "contemplated acts" and "justifiable" are all words that we would use to describe the Executive Functions of the rational brain, rather than something coming from the emotional brain.

So, let's look at how courage ties back to the brain. Clearly, courage has its roots firmly in the fear-based behaviors which tie to the five P's as we have described them, specially the threat-based ones of Protection, Participation and Prediction. While much of courage comes via the form of one's immediate action in crisis, such as those actions of a first responder, we find courage also finds its impact in less acute situations where the brain will run all kinds of scenarios that lead to an over amplification or simplification of a specific fear or group of fears. When courage impacts our sense of our psychological Protection we will often have to stop, assess the situation and acknowledge that our brain will default, at first, to the direst of outcomes given its primary mission of survival. The same is true if Participation or Prediction are the more sensitive of our threats. In all these cases there are opportunities to manage the threat and take action that is rational. Courage then becomes the label we provide to the introduction of a more rational and reasonable response to a situation that, without intervention, is likely to excite our limbic response to nonconscious fears.

Whenever we make a decision or take an action, we are, almost by definition, taking a position or making a stand. Many times, this is relatively easy and does not require us to reflect on our personal values or make value judgments regarding whether the impact of what we do will have serious consequences. Occasionally, we are required to take actions that require us to dig a little deeper – and act in line with our value system. This sometimes means that we have to bring forth that part of us which will make the courageous act.

One final thought; like many emotions, courage tends to be contagious. If just one person sets a courageous example, others will follow.

Culture: It is commonplace these days for organizations to focus on developing a defined culture and recruiting for people who will be a cultural fit. There is, however, a potential trap to this. For example, Creary [33] cautions:

> *"It will be important to question and potentially remove language about "cultural fit" from talent management and performance evaluation processes. Such language can perpetuate racial bias if there isn't consensus on what constitutes cultural fit or if the criteria used to gauge it are biased (for example, grooming or clothing). Instead, leaders can reinforce the values that they think are important to equity and effectiveness and assess "values alignment."*

Diversity and discrimination: Clearly racial diversity and discrimination are not the only manifestations of diversity and discrimination issues. We could have expanded the book to include discrimination and lack of diversity based on weight, age, gender, sexual orientation, religion, etc. Almost anywhere that we can identify a bias, differentiation, faction or label, we can find lack of diversity around those things and discrimination based upon them. Here are a couple of instances where bias and discrimination had serious and direct impacts; a high-school kid who was almost stabbed to death by a classmate during school lunch in a fight that started with him being called skinny and "nerdy;" another kid in middle school that landed in the hospital for weeks after getting repeatedly kicked... because he was overweight.

Empathy: It is a common perception that human beings are endowed with empathy for others. For most of us this is true, but it is not necessarily the case with sociopaths and certain others. It is also not the case that we are equally empathetic for all other people, all of the time. In a famous study, Dr Xu et al [34] demonstrated that while we may <u>say</u> that we have empathy for whomever we see in pain, the empathic neural response in the anterior cingulate cortex (ACC) (that part of the brain that mediates not only first person pain experience but also empathy for others' pain) decreased significantly when participants viewed faces of other races. In other words, their findings uncover neural mechanisms of a built-in empathic bias toward racial ingroup members.

Factions: We first addressed this concept under InGroup Bias. It is, however, such a powerful dynamic, we expand upon it here, and once again, refer back to Roberts and Rizzo [35] for two descriptions:

"People's positive perceptions of themselves often extend to positive perceptions of their group, which leads to ingroup preference."

and

"Because people care about cooperative alliances, they intuitively interpret the groups they are assigned to as requiring cooperation, trust and support, which leads to behaving in ways that benefit the ingroup and are consistent with ingroup norms. Even after being <u>randomly</u> assigned to a minimal group, children and adults feel and express positivity toward their ingroup, associate their ingroup with positivity, empathize with their ingroup, distribute resources in favor of their ingroup, and are far more forgiving of and loyal to ingroup members."

Once again, however, the effect of ingroup behavior can get worse:

"Critically the desire to establish and maintain one's position within a group can also lead individuals to prioritize ingroup loyalty and group norms over moral concerns for fairness and inclusion."

Therefore, as you can see, ingroups can be comforting and reassuring. But they can also provide a means to create factions that pit one group against another, even if that division, at times, goes against what is morally right.

When can that happen? Or, more generally, what about the overall impact of intergroup behavior on racism? Again, from Roberts and Rizzo:

> " ... intergroup tensions are particularly likely to flare when groups experience threats to their self-image, uniqueness, values and beliefs, or goals and resources. Groups also experience threats rooted in intergroup anxiety (i.e. when people are uncertain of how intergroup interactions will play out, they often feel uncomfortable, uneasy and threatened) and negative stereotypes about the group (e.g. when people *expect* outgroups to behave negatively, they experience fear, anger and threat."

It is very easy to see these effects playing out in today's political and social environments in the US.

Fairness: We want to be treated fairly, see others be treated fairly in social and work environments, and we want to see animals treated fairly. It seems that fairness is a very important facet for many people and frequently is identified as the single most important facet.

In summary, as humans we need to see that exchanges that occur around us are fair, both to us and to others. Fair exchanges are intrinsically rewarding to the brain, independent of other factors. When we deem that what we see or experience is unfair, the brain reacts the same way that it does for disgust, one of the six fundamental emotions. On the other hand, when we see or experience activities around us that are fair, our brains react in the same way as if we have been rewarded.

Sarah Brosnan's "Letter to Nature," [36] in connection with capuchin monkeys and perceived unfairness of treatment, describes the results of her work with scientific clarity and brevity. She describes what happens when two monkeys are treated unequally, and it is a stunning show of what happens when these primates observe inequity. The monkey that perceives it is being treated unfairly responds with anger and frustration.

Fairness makes sense from an evolutionary sense. In past eras, if you didn't receive your fair share of the resources of your tribe, then your survival might have been in question.

But before we go any further, let's take a moment and examine what we mean by fairness, especially as it applies to racism and discrimination.

Andreoni et al [37] describe two different aspects of fairness and also how we can change our minds, over relatively short periods of time, about what we believe is fair. They identify the following two approaches: fairness of opportunity vs. fairness of outcomes. Then, when they come to address fairness of outcomes, they talk about whether the outcomes arose out of luck or out of choice. In the case of racism and discrimination, it is easy to see how people of color view their treatment as violating both of these aspects of fairness; what happened to us wasn't fair, and the result isn't fair.

Our experience is that the feeling of fairness (or unfairness) is both highly individual and highly context-driven. From an individual point of view, what is seen as unfair to one person can be judged as fair by another with both of them having equally sound logical and emotional reasoning to support their position. Combine this with the Ladder of Inference from above, and it is easy to see why arguments occur as to whether something is fair or not.

If we consider "social environment" in its largest context, this could be one of the most important issues facing the world today. The fair treatment of one country by another, wars and tension between countries, the fair treatment of refugees, the fair treatment of people of different racial and ethnic backgrounds within a given country, state, or town. The list goes on.

In a 2001 article, [38] Van Den Boss and Lind provide us with a summary of some of the outcomes of fair treatment:

> *"Being treated fairly typically leads to things such as higher commitment to the organization or institution within which the treatment is experienced, more prosocial citizenship behavior, and greater acceptance of authorities. People who experience unfair treatment, on the other hand, are more likely to leave their jobs, show lower levels of commitment, and may even start behaving in antinormative or illegal ways."*

Now let's explore unfairness, in general, and in particular how it combines with the tendency to form ingroups.

When something is seen by our brains as unfair, immoral or unjust, it triggers off the same neural circuitry in the brain as disgust. Disgust is one of the brain's major emotions and is a fundamental survival mechanism. Eons ago, if you weren't disgusted by rotten or decayed objects, then your gene pathway didn't survive. So, for something to trigger off the same circuitry is significant. Unfairness is a powerful sense and drives us both consciously and nonconsciously.

Irrationality: Despite our wonderful brains and the incredible power that they have, we all behave irrationally. There are a number of reasons for this, and many books and papers have been written on each. For example, we may behave irrationally if:

- we see something that is unfair, either to us or to other people.
- specific words or metaphors are used.
- something is framed a certain way.
- something has been "anchored" in our brain.
- we are subject to certain influences.
- our biases are being brought into operation

Unfortunately, much of the time, we are not aware that we are behaving irrationally; the irrational behavior is often the result of something else going on behind the scenes.

Media: It is reasonable to say that, at least in the US, every person is bombarded with messages from the media every day. What those messages say has a direct impact, often nonconscious, on our brains. Whether it be the frequency with which black characters are portrayed on the TV and in movies, or the roles that they play, or the manner in which all characters react to black characters, the media plays a major role in reducing or fostering racism, prejudice and stereotypes.

This portrayal, combined with the brain's natural tendency to shortcut, to anchor, and to be subject to confirmation bias, leads to a formidable dynamic for the brain to overcome.

The backlash against Hollywood's use, portrayal and accolades (or lack thereof) of black actors in 2019 and 2020 is a welcome change versus the exploitation of stereotypes commonly used in years past.

Mega-threats. Leigh and Melwani [39] introduce us to the concept of mega-threats, defined as:

> " ... *large scale, negative, identity relevant occurrences that receive significant media attention.*"

In their article and Leigh's parallel thesis, [40] they opine that there are:

> " ... *psychological consequences of these events – namely anticipatory threat – for event observers that share identity group membership with individual(s) that are attacked, threatened, or harmed in these events and that this experience of threat spills over into the workplace, but in general organizational norms dictate its suppression, leading individuals to engage in a process of emotional and cognitive suppression that (they) characterize as identity labor.*"

In her thesis, Leigh suggests that this threat leads to lower task and social engagement, but that closer work relationships can mitigate this decline to some degree.

Leigh found that women experienced higher levels of anticipatory threat after reading about a mega-threat involving a female victim and that black employees experienced higher levels of anticipatory threat after reading about a mega-threat involving a black victim, and that they anticipated that this threat could have been directed at them.

Make Stuff Up. Our brains are very good at this. And they are very good over a wide range – from filling in missing letters in incomplete words, through to inventing whole explanations as to why a certain person thought the way he/she did. Once we have invented these stories (mostly in the nonconscious part of the brain) our conscious brain gives a rational basis to the story. From then on, we tend to believe what we have made up. When we see something we don't understand, our brains may just make up a very simple explanation, which may help to reinforce easy to remember stereotypes, thus giving the brain yet another short cut.

Positive Deviance. Although the name sounds strange, the concept is very basic and very sound. Let's start with a definition: [41]

"Positive deviance is the observation that in most settings a few at risk individuals follow uncommon, beneficial practices and consequently experience better outcomes than their neighbors who share similar risks."

In other words, maybe there is a work-around or best practice happening right under your nose that can be learned from, copied, or leveraged.

Expanding this definition slightly, Singhal and Svenkerud [42] suggest that part of a general failure in tackling tough issues is a tendency to focus on:

" … outside-in, expert-driven approaches to solving problems and for overlooking and rejecting local solutions."

and the need to:

" … pay more attention to approaches such as positive deviance that enable communities to discover the wisdom they already have and then to act on it. PD is an asset-based approach that identifies what is going right in a community to amplify it, as opposed to focusing on what is going wrong in a community and fixing it with outside expertise. In the PD approach, the change is led by internal change agents who, with access to no special resources, present the social behavioural proof to their peers that problems can be solved. Given that the solutions are generated locally, they are more likely to sustain and be owned by potential adopters."

Translated, this means that in most large enough communities, you will find some examples whereby the issue at hand has been solved. We started to wonder whether, if this is true, a Positive Deviance approach might prove useful in addressing the issue of bias, racism and discrimination.

The bottom line? You may be able to find the solution or at least some useful ideas, if you just look inside your own community or organization.

Some research showed that this thinking had already been applied in some organizations. In their recent article, the title of which starts with *#Black Employees Matter*, Leigh and Melwani [43] describe an approach using Positive Deviance and identify two dynamics which were adopted by Positive Deviants i.e. speaking up on behalf of their group and establishing relationships with other diverse groups. They add that this requires some organizational factors to exist for the success of the approach, i.e. leadership compassion, organizational climate for inclusion, and organizational demography, all of which empower minority employees.

Pre-Frontal Cortex growth. The human prefrontal cortex is one of the last brain regions to mature. Its development starts very early on, and undergoes a variety of developmental spurts during childhood, puberty and early adolescence. It is generally thought, however, that it is not fully formed in humans until the early to mid-twenties, with females maturing earlier than males. Some recent studies suggest that it may be even later. Therefore, we may be subject to more primitive reactions and attitudes when we are young adults and be more able to think rationally as we mature. The downside is that by then many of our biases, habits and values have been well established.

Problems. (p) If we acknowledge that bias, racism, lack of diversity and other associated issues are problems, then it might be useful to understand what type of problems they are. Essentially there are several categories of problems, namely critical problems, general problems and wicked problems. Each requires a different set of thoughts and actions. Critical problems, like there's a fire in the living room, require immediate action and tend to be best addressed by a command-and-control approach. General problems tend to require a thoughtful, planned approach. These are the types of problems that we are faced with day-to-day. How to organize a street fair, how to renovate a house, or how to hold a party. They require planning from start to finish in order to assess what goals to set, what strategies to take and to understand what resources are needed.

Then come wicked problems that are in a class of their own. They have a number of attributes such as:

> It is difficult, or maybe impossible, to define them.
> It is not clear about who "owns" the problem.
> A solution may not exist.
> There are rarely templates to follow.

P There is a more detailed description about problem types in Appendix D.

- There is always more than one explanation for the cause of a wicked problem; the appropriateness of the explanation will depend upon the viewpoint of the explainer.
- There are always many stakeholders involved, all of which has a different interest and a different recommended solution.
- You may never know whether you got it right.
- Taking a step to resolving a wicked problem may make the problem worse.

Addressing wicked problems takes a different mindset. Trying to plan the way through to the end is almost impossible. It requires a high degree of collaboration from a variety of stakeholders, many of whom may be antagonists. It takes a great degree of willingness to adapt an approach.

The impact on the brain of addressing wicked problems is huge. Our brains like things clean, predictable and unambiguous, exactly the opposite of the attributes of a wicked problem.

And, of course, you have guessed it. Racism has all of the attributes of a wicked problem.

Racial trauma. This is a term that seems to have entered the racial lexicon over the past decade, along with the term racial PTSD. They both address the impact of what chronic stress, as a result of racial discrimination, does to the brain. It has generated much research in recent years. One of the leading researchers in this field is Monica Williams whose 2018 paper [44] we use to give us some help in understanding these impacts. First a definition:

"Individual trauma occurs when an event, series of events, or circumstances are experienced by an individual as physically or emotionally harmful or threatening and have lasting adverse effects on the person's functioning and physical, social, emotional, or spiritual well-being."

Williams clarifies some of the impacts:

" … covert discrimination may be equally or more distressing as overt discrimination. Covert discrimination can leave people of color questioning whether an unpleasant interpersonal experience was based on race at all. Much like sexual harassment, ongoing racially discriminatory events can have a cumulative effect that may increase

hypervigilance and avoidance and contribute to PTSD symptoms or the development of a PTSD diagnosis. Trauma-related symptoms such as anxiety, depression, and negative future outlook may be linked to perceived covert discrimination, and as an individual's experience of subtle mistreatment in the form of microaggressions increases so does the predictive relationship with trauma symptoms."

Unfortunately, it gets worse.

"Even if an individual has not experienced a personal trauma, it is believed that a continual fear of race-related stressors and increased paranoia or vigilance may cause traumatization over time or lead to PTSD when accompanied with a more traumatic event. Further, traumatization may be passed down through social and epigenetic mechanisms and just learning about the experiences of others may also contribute through vicarious traumatization. This means that individuals may not need to experience the discrimination at all for it to have an effect."

Let's repeat that last sentence: *"This means that individuals may not need to experience the discrimination at all for it to have an effect."* This supports the mega-threat theory espoused by Leigh and Melwani. So, in addition to trauma from any direct discriminatory events, recipients are subject to additional trauma based upon external, non-experienced factors. As Williams states:

"Racial trauma transcends individual experience, as it includes cultural trauma, which in turn potentiates individual experiences of racial discrimination. The phenomenology of racial trauma may differ from PTSD as it may encompass a wider range of symptoms, such as paranoia, avoidance of dominant group members, somatic complaints, and excessive worries about loved ones."

The conclusion: The impact of chronic racial discrimination can have serious health related issues.

Racism as a health issue. The previous entry gives additional and clear support as to why, as of June 20,2020, more than 20 cities and counties and at least three states, Michigan, Ohio and Wisconsin, have declared racism a public health crisis. [45]

Even with this extra focus, however, there are several problems involved.

First, many therapists and other mental health care practitioners are unaware of the issue of racial trauma or racial PTSD and/or incorrectly diagnose it as another issue.

Secondly, it may be difficult for non-ethnic practitioners to diagnose this and initiate subsequent conversations. According to Williams:

"Assessing discriminatory distress in ethnic minority patients may be uncomfortable for some therapists, particularly European American mental health providers who may feel anxious initiating the topic of racism, despite findings that these conversations can have positive results for clients."

Thirdly, it appears that, at least as of the time this book went to press, there is no agreed-upon measurement process.

Again, Williams:

"This uneasiness with the topic of discrimination could be remedied by assessing distress with a brief, easily administered self-report measure, creating space for therapists to inquire about discriminatory experiences in relation to elevated scores. Importantly, a measure provided to clients, which assesses psychological distress related to discrimination, may improve the overall cultural sensitivity of the therapeutic settings by validating such experiences in affected individuals. Furthermore, such an instrument has the potential to streamline measurement of discriminatory trauma in research settings by assessing the most common symptom areas (i.e., anxiety, emotional distress, and avoidance) found in response to discrimination."

As city, county, state and, dare we hope, national governments, wrestle with their response to this health crisis, overall health issues within ethnic communities have been of major concern for some time. Consider the following: [46]

"The COVID-19 pandemic, according to one study, is killing African Americans at a far greater rate than white Americans. Underlying conditions such as heart disease, diabetes and asthma make people more vulnerable to the virus, and black Americans are more likely to have those diseases than white Americans.

Higher rates of poverty, unemployment, poor housing and toxic environmental exposure, as well as less access to quality medical care also contribute to poor overall health in black communities.

But after class and poverty are accounted for, African Americans still have worse health outcomes than white Americans.

Public health studies have shown that the racism African Americans experience in their daily lives, creates stress that affects their internal organs and overall physical health. This results in a higher prevalence of chronic diseases such as high blood pressure, asthma and diabetes, and a shorter lifespan."

But as this health issue is being discussed at the highest government levels, the implicit bias of even senior medical practitioners makes itself apparent: [47]

"Still some elected officials have questions. Last week, as Ohio lawmakers discussed whether to declare the public health crisis, Republican state Sen. Steve Huffman wondered aloud if more black residents were getting COVID-19 because they have poor hygiene."

"Could it just be that African Americans or the colored population do not wash their hands as well as other groups? Or wear a mask? Or do not socially distance themselves?" said Huffman, who is an emergency room doctor. "Could that be the explanation for why the higher incidence?"

"Huffman clarified that he meant to say, "people of color" rather than "the colored population," and that he had asked the question to further his understanding. His employer, TeamHealth, subsequently fired him."

Segregation: Unfortunately, segregation is widespread across the world. It is often caused by other policies, and, in turn causes other policies in a vicious cycle. Redlining in the US was a classic example of wide-scale segregation, some of the impacts of which can be measured today.

Even in the late 90's segregation was still relatively pervasive, for example, by the use of club memberships. In one small town in the south, approved applicants to join a members-only swimming pool, were disinvited when the approval committee discovered that they were black.

Along with the many injustices that result from segregation, from the brain's perspective it has many impacts. For example, it re-enforces the negative aspects of categorization and ingrouping, and minimizes the opportunity for cross group exchange, one contributor to reducing prejudice and stereotyping. This affects both sides of the racial divide.

Stereotype threats: First an explanation. A stereotype threat occurs:

> " … *when members of a stigmatized group find themselves in a situation where negative stereotypes provide a possible framework for interpreting their behavior, the risk of being judged in light of those stereotypes can elicit a disruptive state that undermines performance and aspirations in that domain.*"[48]

In other words, we induce a self-evaluative internal threat state, if we are part of a group that has negative stereotypes associated with it. This, probably nonconscious, threat state seems to work in three ways:

- like all threats, it physiologically negatively impacts the performance of the Pre-Frontal Cortex
- it distracts the brain by a tendency to constantly worry about and monitor one's actual performance
- it distracts the brain with efforts to suppress negative thoughts and emotions in the service of self-control. [49]

So, it's a little bit like shooting oneself in the foot and can elicit confirmation bias and ultimate attribution error in other observers.

Stress: We are not going to go into a lot of detail about every type of stress here. Dixon and Fitzgerald [50] wrote a complete chapter in their 2020 book; what we will examine here is chronic or toxic stress.

First of all, there are different types of stress; McEwen [51] provides us with a useful classification and explanation, as follows:

> "*Good stress: the experience of rising to a challenge, taking a risk, and feeling rewarded by an, often positive outcome. Healthy self-esteem and good impulse control and decision-making capability, all functions of a healthy brain architecture, are important in this scenario. Even*

adverse outcomes can function as growth experiences for individuals with such positive, adaptive characteristics."

So, not all stress is bad.

"Tolerable stress: situations where negative events occur, but the individual with healthy brain architecture is able to cope, often with the aid of family, friends, and other individuals who provide support. Here "distress" refers to the uncomfortable feeling related to the nature of the stressor and the degree to which the individual feels a lack of ability to influence or control the stressor."

Once again, this stress is not too bad - if you have a healthy brain.

Toxic stress: situations in which negative events are experienced by an individual who has limited support and may also have brain architecture that reflects the effects of adverse early life events that have impaired the development of good impulse control and judgment and adequate self-esteem. Here, the degree and/or duration of distress may be greater. With toxic stress, the inability to cope is likely to have adverse effects on behavior and physiology.

This one is the killer. In specific instances, whether something is perceived as good, tolerable or toxic will depend on many, many factors, including your Personal Threat Profile and Personal Threat Context; indeed, one of the phrases used by McEwen in describing tolerable stress, *"the ability to influence or control the stressor"* directly calls into account Predictability. So, whether you see something as tolerable or toxic, will also depend on your sense of whether you feel the need and ability to influence or control. If this facet of Predictability is not important to you, then a particular stressor may not impact you much. If, on the other hand, your need for influence and control is high, then you may experience a high degree of toxic stress.

If, however, the experience of stress is over a long period of time, say, for example, your life to date if you are a person of color, then the impact can be disastrous from a health point of view; and it doesn't matter whether you are talking physical, emotional or mental health – chronic stress damages them all.

Let's also take a look at the immediate impact of stress on the brain; as we mentioned earlier, one of the reasons that the rational brain (specifically the Pre-Frontal Cortex) is taken "off-line" is perceived, or real threat. Another is tiredness. So, if a person is out late at night, and hence is probably tired, sees a stranger, and perceives them as a threat, then there are several reasons why they will react from the emotional brain, without the rational brain having a dampening or controlling effect. If you now add to the mix that it is a young person, whose Pre-Frontal Cortex is not yet fully formed, we can see the likelihood of increased trouble.

Stranger Danger. When we meet someone new with whom we have no prior knowledge, nothing in common, and no common network connection, then our brain interacts with them as a potential enemy or foe. This makes sense from an evolutionary viewpoint. Millenia ago, strangers were probably not coming around to wish you a nice day! Once we establish a relationship with the new person, typically by finding something in common with them, then the neural circuitry with which we engage with that person changes and we come off our threat edge.

Virtual Reality. Over the past decades there have been many approaches developed with the intent of reducing critical biases with mixed results. There is now some evidence [52, 53] that virtual reality games and digital games may have greater effect on reversing or reducing several important biases, namely, ingroup bias, fundamental attribution error, confirmation bias and bias blind spot, than an equivalent length video training program. Clearly the expense of developing such an approach might be prohibitive for many enterprises, but for wider groups and larger budgets, it might be considered as a possibility and may offer a reasonable ROI.

Chapter Four

Moving Forward

Police Violence

Discrimination

Racial Slurs and Insults

Police Deaths

Racial Profiling

Public Violence

Public Deaths

Death Threats

Redlining

Healthcare

Micro
Injuries

Recruiting
Biases

False Imprisonment

Wealth Inequality

Mass
Incarceration

Educational Discrimination

Racial PTSD and Trauma

Moving Forward

General comments

As we were writing this book, one of our co-authors, Tom, asked the following questions:

> *"If people are shaped by their experiences, how do you create a world that simultaneously recognizes and honors the harm created by those experiences, while trying to create a world where those experiences don't exist…for those already shaped by them? How do we educate and change behavior for those who cause harm? How do we know when those who are harmed can start to lower their defenses? Does the conditioning of all that pain and all that racism make it that much harder to start creating a truly egalitarian world?"*

In response to this, we have put together our collective ideas, together with the best ideas that we have seen in our research. We discovered that the suggestions divided into these areas:

1. What you can do as an individual
2. What you can do to influence someone else
3. What you can do as an enterprise
4. What you can do as a community

Clearly, as one goes down that list, any one of us has less sole and complete control over the impact of these suggestions and the likelihood of them being carried out.

If we are to have an impact on the issue of racism, then we are faced with the prospect of changing the minds of many people, i.e., influencing them. The Forum page of Harper's Magazine in February 2018 commented on this issue and put it in perspective:

> *"Progress is impossible without change" George Bernard Shaw wrote in 1944, "and those who cannot change their minds cannot change anything." But progress through persuasion has never seemed harder to achieve. Political segregation has made many Americans inaccessible, even unimaginable, to those on the other side of the partisan*

divide. On the rare occasions when we do come face-to-face, it is not clear what we could say to change each other's minds or reach a worthwhile compromise. Psychological research has shown that humans often fail to process facts that conflict with our preexisting worldviews. The stakes are simply too high: our self-worth and identity are entangled with our beliefs – and with those who share them. The weakness of logic as a tool of persuasion, combined with the urgency of the political moment, can be paralyzing."

If we are going to change worldviews that have become entrenched over centuries, it is imperative that we find a different approach to influencing other people. We dare not succumb to the old adage of "The definition of insanity is doing the same thing again and expecting a different result." That admonishment would be true at any time but is particularly relevant in today's political, racially entrenched, environment.

Hence, we needed, and deliberately looked for, a different way of going about addressing the issue – thus the brain-based approach.

In each of the five layers, (individual change, influencing others, enterprise approach, community change, national initiative), we offer a number of ideas and thoughts, and we do so by way of a story. The suggestions in the story are offered in no particular sequence. We are all different. What works for one person might not work for another; and what works for one person in one situation might not work in a different one. We offer these simply as suggestions; they have arisen from the work that we have done, the reading that we have done and the interviewing that we have done. For those that are interested, but don't want to read the short stories, a bulleted list of ideas is included in Appendix H.

We also wanted to offer specific things to do rather than generalized strategies, although where we thought it useful, we have added some of those.

What we do know about change is that large change is often the result of lots of small changes. So, moving forward, do what you can to change what you can, at whatever level you can. If you cannot change something, then do what you can to influence it. And if you cannot change it or influence it, then don't waste your time and energy - move on and find something that you can change or influence.

Although it might seem trite to use the excuse "Rome wasn't built in a day," but change on this scale will take time. That truism applies regardless of whether you are attempting change at the individual level, the enterprise level, or the community level. In all cases the progress will probably be frustratingly slow.

In our section on other influences on the brain, we identified that the issue of racism is a wicked problem, and as such presents a series of challenges with regard to how we go about solving it. What we do know about solving wicked problems is that the solutions involve many stakeholders, working together, with a great amount of persistence; they need to be willing to try new things and change their approach when they have learned what does and doesn't work.

We also know that large change tends to start with lots of small changes, and small changes start when one or more people do something different, even if only slightly different. Change starts when one or more individuals change their thoughts and do something different one day than what they did the previous day. This will require their brains to adopt a change; hence we recommend using a brain-based lens to review any suggested approach. More explicitly, we recommend reviewing how the brains of every stakeholder might react to any specific approaches.

And large change takes time. Any significant overall impact will probably take a multi-generational change effort. We need to educate every generation at every given point in time.

a) <u>What you can do as an individual.</u>

As we were concluding the main thrust of writing this book, we read an article in CNN [54] in which Prince Harry described his "awakening" to systemic racism, saying "the world that we know has been created by white people for white people."

Prince Harry said he has only recently recognized the full extent of racism in everyday life, telling the UK's Evening Standard newspaper: "I've had an awakening as such of my own, because I wasn't aware of so many of the issues and so many of the problems within the UK, but also globally as well. I thought I did but I didn't."

This is a great example of someone who was unaware and is willing to learn. But we decided to go one step further and imagine what we would do if we were Prince Harry, having had that light bulb come on. So, this is our fictitious account of what Prince Harry did next. We have taken the liberty of writing it in the first person.

. . . .

Having reached that insight, I decided I needed to increase my awareness of racism as an issue and how it plays out, both explicitly and implicitly, in the day to day lives of people of color, and how the rest of us impact that. I started reading books, I read some scholarly articles and Meghan and I started watching movies together and discussing the implications. [q] *We read Jason's book and used what it contains as a guide.*

In particular, we both decided to increase our knowledge of another race or ethnic group. Once again books, articles and movies provided a good starting point. But we wanted to go further. Meghan, of course, had an advantage over me, but I was determined to learn. I knew that I could never fully live her experience or that of any person of color, but I knew I could learn to be an ally.

I thought a first step would be to fully understand myself, my own biases, habits, anchors, and patterns. I went one step further and looked at these mental models both when I was sitting in the cold light of day, and when I was under stress, to see the difference. It soon became obvious

---

q We have provided some suggestions in Appendix F

to me that my nonconscious mental models were far more pronounced, and had much greater impact on my thinking, when I was under stress than when I was calm. I resolved to get better at stress management.

I discovered the IAT's [r] offered by Harvard's Project Implicit. These tests help show your implicit attitude about a given subject, e.g. race, gender, guns etc. that you did not know about, and bring it to your attention. They helped me identify where I had nonconscious biases.

Meghan and I discussed the fact that most of us don't feel comfortable having conversations about this sensitive topic. I determined to summon up the moral courage to learn how to engage in productive conversations about race. I knew that it would require effort and would best be done by speaking with people that I hadn't spoken to before.

Now that was easier said than done. How did I go about having these conversations? First, I realized that I had to be honest with myself. I acknowledged that it was okay for me to have no idea how to have these conversations about race or how to even start one. I read that one of the things that so many white people think, or are taught, is that not talking about race is the primary method to promote in a non-racist state of being. That had, indeed, been my mental model. I now realized that the problem with this "out of sight, out of mind" approach is that I literally had no point of reference for having the race conversation. The fear in my mind was "Well, I don't want to offend anyone." Meghan helped me understand that my silence was just as offensive as the words I was scared to use.

So, I contacted Jason. He suggested that I start the conversation with a simple, "I don't know what to say, but I want to learn more." He did warn me – be honest and be sympathetic.

Jason educated me about a common mistake. It appears that there is a common belief that, if you are a white person, then you can simply go to your friend of color and ask them to educate you. This sounds good in theory, but if you are coming to your friend of color during a particularly emotional period...like, maybe, immediately after the murder of George Floyd, then it is safe to assume that you will probably need to get in line. There's a high likelihood that every white

---

[r] IAT = Implicit Association Tests

person orbiting your friend of color's life is asking the same questions that you want to ask. Your friend of color is likely to be emotionally drained, because on top of having to be the "Google of the Black Experience For all Of My White Friends" they also have to work, love their partner, raise their kids, pay their bills, deal with their own emotional grief over the state of race relations in the country, eat, sleep, and do all of their normal range of daily activities; then they need to get up and do it all over again the next day.

Jason advised me that if I was going to approach my friend of color, gaining some knowledge of the issue in advance would progress the conversation much further forward.

I decided that I was going to keep a journal; my Ladder of Learning journal. I gradually recognized more and more of the hidden aspects of bias, racism and discrimination.

Jason also suggested that I might review how I had behaved in the past when faced with unpleasant, biased or discriminatory behavior. He said, with a grin, that maybe it was in the grocery line, or the gas station, or at work, or in a restaurant, or in a shop. He knew that, with my somewhat elevated past, I was unlikely to have experienced those things. But he was gentle and described that thinking about past behavior would help determine how I might want to behave in the future and suggested that I practice an alternative response in my mind.

He talked to me about ingroups and outgroups. He described that most of us have several ingroups that we belong to, and those ingroups impact how we see ourselves, how we see other members of our ingroup and how we tend to view people who are not in our ingroup. He asked me to think on how other outgroups view my ingroup?

Earlier on, I said that, although I could not experience what Meghan had experienced, I could learn how to become an ally. To this end, I decided to adopt the L.E.A.P model which Jason had told me about; Listen, Engage, Ask and Provide support.

. . . .

Take a moment and reflect upon the first steps that you might take to more fully understand this issue and prepare yourself for moving forward.

b) **What you can do to influence someone else**

How many of us are actually aware of how we typically go about influencing others? Please note that we say, "influencing others," and do not say, "changing others." You cannot change other people – only they can make that decision. You can only change yourself and how you interact with, and react to, others. However, we all have an opportunity, almost on a daily basis, to influence others. But how is it best for you, in particular, to go about that process? What are your strengths that can be brought to bear? How can you best leverage those strengths?

Take a moment and reflect upon the times you have successfully influenced someone else in the past. What worked? To what degree can you use that approach again?

What about when you attempted to influence someone and failed? How would you about it differently next time?

In the context of influencing other people's thoughts about racism, we think it is important to recognize the distinct difference between ignorance and malevolence. Some people act the way they do, not out of hatred, but out of not knowing any better, or not having given the issue much thought. The example we gave in the previous section about Prince Harry is a case in point. Let's focus on the many Prince Harrys in the world. On the other hand, of course there are people who have simply made up their minds, and nothing will influence them. We recommend focusing on the former, not the latter; be selective on when and where to have these conversations, and with whom. You will not be able to influence everybody. Focus on those people that give an indication that they are ready, willing and able to change and channel your energy into the people that are likely to change. Wasting your energy on people who are clearly entrenched in their views is only going to frustrate you and them, and is very unlikely to change anything in a positive direction.

Think back on a time when you tried to persuade someone and realized that their viewpoint was so embedded that you were wasting your time. How did you become aware that it was a futile effort?

Avoid telling people what to do. Or using any form of speech that might be perceived as telling them what to do. For example, "You should" type of phraseology or "You need to" type of advice will get you into almost as much trouble. You may recall from our section on the brain that, in general, we hate to be told what to do. Most of us want to feel independent and we want to have control over our own destiny – or at least the perception of control. So, what should we do instead of telling people what to do? Use different words and phrases that might be a little more brain-friendly like "Would you consider …. ?" or "Would you be open to … ?"

> If you were wanting to suggest a different approach that someone else might take, how would you go about it, avoiding telling them what to do?

Look at your own level of courage; there will be many courageous acts that we will all be required to execute as we start to address this issue. Read some of the ways in which you can learn how to be courageous without being foolhardy. [s]

> How courageous do you feel in having direct conversations about the issues of bias, racism and discrimination? What could you do to increase your courage?

Remember "the activist's dilemma." The very acts that raise awareness of a situation can be the same acts that reduce public support for your efforts. Develop a balanced approach and always keep the long-term aim in mind.

When presenting an idea or approach, especially if you are going to use data to support your argument, remember the framing effect (See page 104 for an explanation). The way in which you frame something can significantly impact the brain of the person listening, either positively or negatively. In some cases, just framing the data the wrong way can have the opposite impact to what you intended.

> We all have natural tendencies to approach things the same way we always have. To what degree is your approach effective in reaching a balance?

Influencing people is both a science and an art. To truly influence someone, you need to focus on both parts of the brain; you will need to appeal to both the

---

[s] Some ways to develop courage are given in Appendix E

emotional brain and the logical brain. Present the logical data and information by all means, but don't miss out on the emotional appeal.

In addition, remember that people's brains are drastically impacted by the first things you say – those first words set the stage. For example, if you are trying to persuade someone to donate to a cause, starting out with a large, but impossible number, will, in general result in a greater contribution than starting low. Imagine saying "I know that it won't be possible for you to manage the hundred thousand dollars but what would be affordable for you?"

Also remember that people are more likely to be persuaded by you if they like you, trust you and believe you have credibility. And these factors need to be established in advance. In many cases, this can be achieved by identifying something in common with the other person.

> To what degree do you ensure that your approach includes a focus on both parts of the brain? Do you have a mechanism to quickly establish something in common.?

c) <u>What you can do as an enterprise</u>

Before making any suggestions, we wanted to clarify that what we mean by an enterprise is any group of people working towards a common goal. This might mean a business, a school, a church, a restaurant, a club etc.

We also wanted to offer a couple of examples that illustrate enterprises that have already taken some practical steps to address the issue using, maybe, some more unusual approaches:

Take for example, the television series, the Voice. They eliminate the possibility of being influenced visually by having the judges face the opposite way before deciding whether to select an auditioning person. And many symphony orchestras have started to do something similar when auditioning new members. They eliminate visual bias by having them audition behind a curtain.

We also decided that we would take a similar story-based approach: let our imagination run wild and think about what the ideal large organization would do, told in a story as if we were the CEO of that large organization.

. . . .

Once the issue of systemic racism had come to the forefront of my mind, I decided to act on it immediately. I knew that our organization needed a top-to-bottom review.

Clearly, I had to start at the top, with myself and my team. I understood from my reading that many change efforts in organizations fail, and I determined that we were not going to be one of them. We would succeed. Furthermore, I knew that many Diversity and Inclusion efforts fail because senior executives are unwilling to become the first; the first to become aware, the first to admit their mistakes and honor past injustices, the first to say sorry, the first to be educated, the first to change or the first to become role models. I was determined not to fall into those traps. So, I called in Jason, my CHRO, Mary, and her advisors, to help me craft a manifesto. I wanted everyone in the organization to know that I was taking this seriously and that we would expend resources on all associated initiatives. Jason showed me one written by the CEO of Korn Ferry, Gary Burnison, and I was impressed. I wanted something equally as powerful. [t]

I was encouraged to be transparent and specific about what we were going to implement, and, where possible, make clear what we were going to do. We needed for our approach to be measurable and hold ourselves accountable for getting results. I was also advised that I would increase the chance of success if we were authentic and really taking action for the right reasons. Even our General Counsel said that we needed to be in earnest and not just check a box, quiet the noise, or avoid a lawsuit. I was a little uncertain about being completely transparent as, in many areas, we didn't initially know what we were going to do. So, what was the advice that I was given? Be upfront about those areas but tell the organization when we would get back to them with some more detail.

I had read that one of the reasons that large-scale cultural change efforts fail, is that they don't have a powerful, senior team putting their weight behind the effort. Once again Mary and her advisors helped me to pull together a group to shepherd the effort, with me as part of that group. We made a commitment of senior level leadership time over the next five years. In support of this commitment, we are in the process of recruiting a Chief Diversity Officer.

The first thing that the team did was to become aware; aware of our own mental models. Aware of what the best practices were. Aware of the current situation, both within our enterprise, within our surrounding communities and within the countries in which we did business. We brought in experts in a variety of fields. We each took the IAT's. We each received help from trained coaches to help us understand our own biases, anchors, habits and patterns.

We appointed one of the team members to be responsible for communicating what we were doing to the rest of the organization. He laid out an overall communication plan using many different types of media; email, videos, zoom calls, town hall meetings, webinars, guest speakers, focus groups, working groups, lunches with the CEO and many more. I was given a list of random employees to phone with whom to have a brief discussion. Within a couple of weeks, I could feel that the organization had taken on a new dynamic – the change was palpable.

---

[t] Gary Burnison's CEO statement is reproduced in Appendix G as an example of such an approach.

We had recruited someone from the Project Management Office to help guide us through the many things that had to get done. She and the VP of Diversity identified an explicit set of objectives, strategy, initiatives and metrics. Then they laid out a plan for us that included company-wide initiatives to build awareness, to educate, to review blind-spots and barriers, and to do process and culture reviews.

One of the first items in the plan was for me to publicly acknowledge the past and apologize for areas that were clearly wrong. I did so in a company-wide live-stream video saying that while we may as well give up hope for a better yesterday, that we would ensure that tomorrow would be forged differently. We also decided that it was important to establish where we were at the beginning of our journey, so we established qualitative and quantitative benchmarks thinking that it would be better to be able to measure something over time in order to know whether the initiatives that we were taking were having the desired effect. In addition, that process of monitoring where we were and how we were improving, made it easier to celebrate the small victories.

After just a couple of meetings of the team, it became apparent that this culture change would involve almost every aspect of the enterprise and that all of the changes would need to be done in concert so that they were in alignment. It was emphasized to me that doing Diversity, Equality, Inclusion and Impact training was an important and necessary step, but has been demonstrated to have mixed results and, in most cases, has not been shown to have major impact in the long term; it needs to be reinforced from all other aspects of the enterprise. Every system, structure, policy, procedure and process needed to be reviewed and changed so that they support the desired end result.

I expected that the team and I would go through a lot of training ahead of everyone else in the company. I was a little surprised that the first set of training programs that we attended weren't about Diversity and Inclusion. They were about listening and asking powerful questions. They set us up to hear what was actually being told to us rather than confirming what we wanted to hear.

And I don't mind admitting that some of what I heard over the following months was a little disturbing. I had no idea that had been going on in the organization. But that did provide the *foundation for me to go back on live-stream, apologize and make sure people knew that we would not tolerate those behaviors anymore.*

I was sure that we would then be educated in the issues of Diversity and Inclusion, but I was wrong. We were then given practice in collaboration and coalition building across diverse situations. The combination of listening, questioning and learning how to collaborate was very powerful. I started to wonder why I had not been exposed to all of this much, much earlier in my career.

The good news was that in the process of listening and asking probing questions, we found out that there were parts of the organization that seemed to have most of the issues solved. We were able to reach into those areas and identify some champions and evangelists that we could use as ambassadors as the change gained momentum.

We were guided that it is easier to make a small change than a larger one, and when small changes have taken ahold, it is more likely that a larger change will be adopted. It was also strongly suggested that we explicitly and publicly celebrate small positive changes.

Jason suggested that as human beings we are notoriously bad at identifying our own biases. In fact, ironically, one of our biases is our tendency to be able to identify bias in other people. So, he suggested that teaming up with another person can help us identify and address our own biases, habits tendencies and patterns. We called them bias buddies.

As we started to address biases in the organization, we asked each manager to identify the ingroups that they belonged to, or knew about, in their departments. Then we asked them what impacts, both positive and negative, those ingroups had in the areas of racism and discrimination. We discovered some interesting cases. Most were apparently benign but led to a sense of resentment. One manager, always went to lunch with the people he knew and rarely, if ever, took a new employee to lunch. Another small group met twice a week, early in the morning, and payed racquetball together, often making business decisions as they did so.

Jason and Mary guided us that, in this process, people would likely be taken out of their comfort zone. This was a necessary step. They also insisted that all of their programs keep people feeling safe. They pointed out that our brains can't learn anything if they feel threatened or defensive. All of the programs that they developed were structured so as to optimize the likelihood of learning taking place. I remember one conversation where they asked whether, in my younger days as a manager, I had ever been made to sit in day long training programs. They asked me to rate how effective they were. Needless to say, I confirmed their hypothesis that we need to be engaged to learn, and one of the best ways is to appeal to people's curiosity.

It wasn't all sweetness and light, by any means. At one point, several months into our journey, one of our junior staff members had been explaining what we were doing to a number of her fellow members in a club she belonged to. She was telling them how proud she was of the positive actions we were taking. To her, and our surprise, she received a lot of pushback and negative comments. She, and we, had naively assumed that our initiatives would be welcomed by all. That caused us to also look outside of our own organization and get more involved in the communities in which we had offices and stores. We also reached out to other like-minded organizations and developed an informal inter-organizational group to exchange ideas. Doing this was a very powerful step in that it provided us with other best-practice ideas that we would not have come up with on our own. It taught us some lessons as well. What works in one company or organization doesn't always transfer to another. One value-added step we took was to reach out to several local universities to see what we could learn from the academics. They were very willing to share their knowledge, and over time, we became the subjects for several of their breakthrough studies.

One of the other areas where we nearly stubbed our organizational toe, was in the area of culture. We have been, and still are, proud of the culture that we have built up over the years. What we hadn't realized, however, was that some of the very things we were proud of, were some of the things that were embedding discrimination. For example, we had policies on hair, tattoos and beards, all put in place in the past to avoid upsetting our customers. A quick review identified that they were very likely discriminatory. We did an explicit review of all of the cultural aspects of every system in our organization. We discovered that our recruitment and promotional processes were very vulnerable and needed significant revision.

Mary and her staff did a large number of interviews and found that probably our single biggest point of vulnerability was in our onboarding process. We slowly began to realize that we needed to get it right from the start. Since we had a reasonably high degree of turnover, it was important to start at the beginning of an employee's life cycle with the company. We needed to ensure that new employees fully understood where the enterprise stood with respect to bias and racism. We developed a completely separate module as part of our on-boarding and orientation program.

It probably goes without saying that, early on, we establish a Diversity council. We identified people who we knew were passionate about the subject, but we didn't restrict ourselves to just those people. We included people who were well-respected as informal leaders. We included people who had shown themselves to be evangelists for various causes. We included people who had shown that they were positive agents for change. And we gave the council authority.

One of the first things that the council did was to establish an independent external diversity/ethics hotline. They recommended that it was directly handled by the Chief Diversity Officer – and that that person had direct access to me. We have appointed a Diversity sub-committee at the Board of Directors level; in the same manner that the Finance sub-committee relies on external auditors, we are in the process of identifying an external diversity audit group to assist us.

In addition, the council, together with HR, changed the way that we set performance goals; now DBIE goals must be included in every manager's performance reviews, and the goals must adhere to the S.M.A.R.T. approach of goal-setting. We are in the process of identifying these DBIE goals and guidelines, which will be both quantitative and qualitative. We will be linking the pay, pay increases, promotions and bonuses to performance against those guidelines by all senior managers and executives.

In one of the many conversations I had with Jason, Mary and her team, we focused on traps. We knew that we would make mistakes, but there were some that we could clearly avoid, even though they might not be immediately obvious.

For example, we knew that we needed to create safe spaces for leaders, managers, and employees so they could be upfront about any issues and/or concerns that they may have before embarking on some of these new initiatives. Mary described a common situation. Many white managers have not led diverse teams, nor do they have many, if any, friends of color in their personal lives. So, the idea of effectively being in charge of the career of someone they do not understand on a professional and personal level is daunting. As a result, what managers will often do is to attempt to make the employee in their image, thus forcing them inside of their ingroup with no clear appreciation for what the employee actually needs. We paid extra attention to this type of situation and gave the manager extra coaching.

On the other side of that equation is the employee, who is coming to the proverbial table with their own concerns about the arrangement. Perhaps this is their first time being managed by someone white; perhaps their last experience with a white manager was problematic, which will in turn bring a large degree of uncertainty, fear and anxiety, especially if they are unable to meet the imposed standards of a leader who is dealing with her own set of anxieties. We offered specific and explicit training for all stakeholders on how to deal with these situations.

This led to a longer discussion: What should we do in advance when a leader, who happens to be white, is assigned an employee of color to mentor and develop? Jason and Mary both offered words of caution in that, from their experiences this arrangement often failed in spectacular fashion, for a number of reasons. Maybe, the leader/employee pairing was just a poor fit in the first place; the employee may have been promoted before they were ready for the responsibilities involved in a management track. Maybe the manager wasn't equipped with basic skills such as self-awareness, directness, and honesty. No one, especially a white male, wants to be perceived as a racist. Therefore, they will "grin and bear it" when given the assignment of grooming a diverse employee for further development. What they are not being honest about is their overall sense of discomfort in working with someone they may have little to nothing in common with, in addition to the fear that they are going to say or do something culturally offensive. Once again, we were overly cautious when faced with this situation and gave extra training and coaching, to both the manager and the employee.

One final thing that we are considering for the organization – an Employee Bill of Rights. We're not sure what it will contain, but it's starting to form in the minds of myself and the Diversity Council.

As I said at the beginning, I was determined that we would make our change effort succeed and we would not become yet another failure statistic. I think we addressed most things in a sensitive and logical way. Time will tell.

. . . .

If you had a magic wand and were called in to advise your CEO and senior team, what would be the first steps that you would recommend your organization implement?

In your organization, what would be the best way to communicate what the DBEI initiative was and how it was going to be implemented?

As you look back in your own organization, what specific things have not been handled well in the past? What should be done by way of an apology? What else should be done?

As you look at your own organization, what systems, structures, policies, procedures and processes need to be revised in order to bring about a more equitable environment?

How good are the managers and leaders in your organization at listening and asking probing, powerful questions? What needs to be improved?

How good are the managers and leaders in your organization at collaborating and building coalitions across departments? What needs to be improved?

Where, in your organization have people already adopted a more equitable approach? What can be learned from them?

How good is your organization at celebrating small changes and wins?

What ingroups do you see in your organization? What is their impact?

What are the most effective training approaches for your organization?

What other enterprises could you engage with?

How does the culture of your organization support diversity, equality and inclusion? What gets in the way?

d) <u>What you can do as a community</u>

Once again, we thought that it would be useful for us to give a definition of what we mean by community, in general and what we are going to focus on. By community, in general, we mean everything from a local small-town community, over which any one individual may actually have some influence, through to the national or societal level, over which we have little to no influence as individuals other than via the polling booth. So, in this section we are going to focus on what a local, small-town community can do. It seems a more reasonable starting point.

But first, we would like to point you back to the previous sections on what you might do as an individual, how you might influence others and what you can at the enterprise level and use some of those ideas as a starting point.

In a similar fashion to before, we decided we would let our imagination run wild again, and we set up a fictitious town hall meeting. There are approximately thirty concerned citizens that are in conversation with the mayor and the police chief. We join them in the middle of the meeting; one of the citizens has just asked the mayor what the town council is proposing to actually do:

. . . .

Mayor: The first thing that we decided to do, and have already put in motion, is a complete review of all our policies and procedures with a view to ensuring that there are no built-in biases or prejudices in the way that they work and the way that they are written up. We are using some outside consultants who are experienced in what to look for.

Let me give you an example of something we are looking at. Our culture and dress-code. Now who would have thought that we would have discrimination there? But until recently we had a policy that no beards and no tattoos were allowed. The consultants pointed out that that can be discriminatory for certain races and religions.

So, as I said in my opening remarks, the very fact that we're here having this conversation, I hope gives weight when I say that we are aware, that we are listening, and to the best of our ability, we will act.

Police Chief: And we are following suit, doing the same thing with all of our policies, processes and procedures. Especially in our advertising, recruiting and promotional practices.

Citizen 1: And when will these reviews be finished and how will we find out about the results?

Police Chief: We are planning to have our review wrapped by the end of next month; we'll hold another meeting like this to let everyone know what we found out.

Mayor: Likewise, we are targeting the end of next month, but it looks like we might be running a week or so late. Mike and I will come before you as soon as both reports are finished and available. We will put the reports on our FaceBook page and make copies available in the local library and on the tables in the entry hall to the Town Hall for anyone that wants one. We were looking at mailing a hard copy to everyone in town but that proved too costly. We think there are better ways to spend the town's money.

Citizen 2: We claim that we are an integrated town, but I still see major divisions. What steps are you taking to increase our integration?

Mayor: We have just kicked off some initiatives in that direction. First, I am personally going to run a Diversity Council consisting of a mixture of town officials and volunteers to see what we have to do in the way of greater integration. Second, we have initiated a joint task force with three of the local hospitals and other health care providers to look at how we should address past and present issues of health care. We're hoping that the outcome of this task force will examine the current issues regarding equal access to health care facilities together with the past impact of racism as a health care issue. Third, we are in the process of initiating a public-private investment fund for small businesses. Finally, we are meeting with three of the local universities and colleges, for them to revise their health care, nursing and therapy training, to include the issue of stress and racism as a health care issue. In connection with this last effort we are looking at ways to increase outreach so that all citizens can get mental health care treatment at no cost.

Citizen 2: That's all very interesting, but how does the average person like me get involved?

Mayor: There will be an open enrollment opportunity on the website asking for volunteers.

Citizen 2: *What if I don't have access to the Internet?*

Mayor: *There will be forms available at the Town Hall lobby, the County Hall and all of the libraries. It will take a couple of weeks, but we will have them there as soon as we can.*

Police Chief: *If I can add, the Mayor and I are going to write a weekly column for the local paper, and it will be focused on bias, racism and discrimination and how to reduce them and their impact. We know that it will take time, but we want to establish as many avenues as possible to hold conversations about the issues. We have already installed an independent hotline for complaints, and we will publicize that number. Last month, the council approved the establishment of an independent, citizen-driven investigation unit.*

Citizen 3: *If I may, I would like to add something to the conversation. As many of you know, I am the President of the local community college. We have received a large donation from a local business to drive an outreach program for education into poorer communities. I will be establishing a task force and will be looking for volunteers to join us. We will, of course, be working in concert with the Mayor and the Police Chief to coordinate our efforts.*

Mayor: *Thank you. That is great to hear. What other questions are there?*

Citizen 4: *What about unconscious bias training for everyone who works for the town and everyone who works in law enforcement?*

Mayor: *I am sorry I forgot that. We started that several months ago. It seems to be having some results but its early days yet.*

Police Chief: *I agree with the Mayor. We are running all of our staff and all of our street officers through a similar training, although, in addition, there's a large focus on de-escalation in our training. As the Mayor stated, it's early days, but so far so good. We're getting good feedback on the training itself although we're not complete yet.*

Mayor: Let me come back to the local paper for a moment. One of the things that we will be emphasizing in our column is the danger of passivism. We want to encourage people, like it says in the airports. If you see something, say something. I think, in the past, we have all let acts of abuse and discrimination pass us by, or we have turned a blind eye to them. Well, we need to put an end to that habit. Let's all agree that if we see something, we do something about it. Or take it to someone that can do something about it.

We all know that this is a problem that has been around for a long time and will take a concerted effort to resolve. The Police Chief and I, and many others, are resolved to tackle it and will do so one step at a time.

. . . .

Acknowledgments

As always with books like this, looks can be deceiving. There is always a lot more that goes on behind the scenes than just what is done by the authors. Guidance, ideas, support, proof reading, counselling, consulting, editing, cups of tea - the list goes on. So, thank you to everyone who helped.

Specifically, we would like to call out a few names in particular:

Phil:

Scott Fitzgerald has been Phil's co-author in two previous books, and while he was not explicitly an author of the book, he contributed in a number of ways. He partook in numerous discussions about the topic, gave sage counsel, encouraged us to take a broad and gentle approach, and provided constant support.

Jackie Sergent, the mayor of the town that Phil lives in, for her support and encouragement from the very beginning of the project. Thank you, Jackie.

Thank you, Jessica van Schie, one of Phil's god-children, for proof-reading early versions of the book. Thank you, Rita Campbell, for proof-reading later versions.

Thank you, Larry Kuznar, Sabrina Polansky, Allison Astorino-Courtois, some of Tom's colleagues, for their intellectual thoughts around this and many other topics.

Susan Larson Kidd provided much needed intellectual and emotional support and encouragement from when the book was simply a concept through to the very end.

Early on in the process, Nancy Hauge, an eminent CHRO, challenged the very concept of DEI – Diversity, Equity and Inclusion – saying that it was lacking in a couple of ways. The first thing she suggested that it was lacking something about having Impact. So, we added that. Then she suggested that Inclusion still had some connotations to it, and that maybe Belonging was a better term. Hence DBIE – Diversity, Belonging, Impact and Equity. Thank you, Nancy, for that, for your support and for many other discussions.

Peter and Karen Johnson, for wide-ranging discussions on this and many related and unrelated topics over many glasses of wine and gin and tonics at the Lark Farm Gin and Tonic center.

Andrea Hill, a beautiful, smart, African American leader in the Hooters organization for her courage, tenacity and drive in pushing this topic to front and center.

Ryan Carey, of BetterOn, for his enthusiasm and support, and for helping people of all backgrounds realize their own presence and purpose through the lens of the video camera.

Gabrielle Barber, better known as Gabby, provided invaluable administrative, logistical, software and publishing support from soup to nuts – and in a focused get-it-done manner.

Maybe it goes without saying that each of the three co-authors, would mutually thank each other. In my, Phil's, case I would like to thank Tom and Jason in separate ways. Tom, for his thoughtful, candid and insightful suggestions. His comments added great value to the resulting manuscript. Jason for the emotional courage to recount his stories for us to share and for bringing the sorry state of racism in America to my, and all of our, attention.

Last, but by no means least, I would like to thank my wife, Cathy for her support, feedback, proof-reading and allowing me the space to take most of the summer of 2020 in my office in order to produce this book

Jason

I want to thank my parents, Dr. Jerome and Elaine Greer, for everything. You sacrificed so many things to raise and guide me. One of the greatest honors in my life is being your son and I love you so much.

To my wife Tiffany…who would've thought that a chance encounter at Valparaiso University way back in 1996 would lead to a lifetime of love, friendship and adventure. You have given me far more than I could ever repay, and I am proud to say that I love you. Thank you for everything.

Brenda Bacon, my matriarch, you challenged me to believe in myself in 2007. I literally would not be in this position if you and my brother in arms, Dan Lawson, had not taken a chance on me. I will always be grateful to you.

Julian Johnson, the conversation we had back in 2016 will always stay between the two of us, but you saved me that day and you reminded me to always trust in God's plan for my life. Thank you, my brother.

I have so many people that have poured life into me over the years. Mr. Hippenbecker, Mrs. Peggy Simmons, Professor Walton, Professor Petties, Mr. Mueller, Phillip and Mary Wright, Michael Beebe, Mrs. Ijei, Cole Simon, Cathy Dixon, Annette Lewis, Jeremy Edwards and Colin Anthony.

Last but not least, I would like to acknowledge my co-author, Phil Dixon and his wife Cathy. Phil and Cathy, I cannot even begin to properly describe the impact that you have had on me. My life is better because you are in it and you will always be my "big brother and big sister." I love the both of you!

Appendices

Appendix A: List of Threat & Reward Facets

Driving Force #1: Protection

1. We want to feel physically safe.

2. We want to feel emotionally safe in our personal, our work, and our social relationships.

3. We want to feel financially secure and avoid financial loss.

4. We want a balance between short-term rewards and long-term gains.

5. We want to know where we stand – geographically and in our social and work relationships.

6. We want to be treated fairly, see others be treated fairly in social and work environments, and see animals treated fairly.

7. We want to be treated as equals in our primary relationships and see other people treated as equals in their primary relationships.

8. We want to feel resilient, i.e., we want to be able to bounce back from life's troughs.

9. We want to be and feel healthy – physically, mentally, emotionally, and spiritually.

Driving Force #2: Participation

10. We want to be trusted, be trustworthy, and be with people we trust.

11. We want to be with people with whom we have something in common, with whom we belong and feel accepted, and who we like.

12. We want to differentiate ourselves from the group and be able to proffer different or even oppositional viewpoints from the group.

13. We want to work on a team – or some of us do.

14. We want a sense of self-respect and self-esteem, to feel equal to or better than others, and see life as a competition where we want to win or beat other people.

15. We want to receive recognition from people who are important to us, be valued and respected by them, know that they care about us, and know that we have some level of approval from them.

16. We want some sense of power and influence in our work and our social lives.

17. We want some sense of status and prestige in our work and our social lives.

18. We want to treat other people in a benevolent fashion.

19. We want to avoid looking incompetent/stupid.

20. We want to avoid feeling like an imposter/fraud.

Driving Force #3: Prediction

21. We want to have some degree of certainty about the future and be clear at work and in our social lives.

22. We want to know what is expected of us in our work and social lives.

23. We want to know how we will be measured and evaluated.

24. We want to know how we will be rewarded.

25. We want to have a high degree of autonomy, i.e., be in control of our own destiny, in our work and in our social lives.

26. We want to make things happen in our work life and in our social life.

27. We want to know what's going on.

28. We want to be right and achieve some degree of perfectionism.

29. We want no changes – keep things the same at work and in our social lives.

30. We want to understand what is going on and make sense of things at work and socially.

31. We want things to be consistent.

32. We want some ambiguity in work and social situations – but not too much.

33. We want some things to be spontaneous, but surprises at work and socially can scare us.

34. We want to feel that we can take care of ourselves.

35. We want to have some sense of tradition.

36. We want to have some sense of conformity.

37. We want to have some sense of harmony and stability at work and socially.

38. We want to be sure – we don't like feeling doubt.

39. We want people to be authentic with us.

40. We want to minimize risk at work and in our social lives.

41. We want to be curious and learn.

42. We want to know that we are heard and our opinions count.

43. We want to be able to "go with the flow" at work and in social situations.

44. We want to have commitment from others at work and from others in our social lives.

Driving Force #4: Purpose

45. We want to achieve mastery in our fields and have an opportunity to practice it on a regular basis.

46. We want to develop ourselves/self-actualize.

47. We want to have a Mission/Purpose and know that our lives have Meaning.

48. We want to live in accordance with our core values and work with people/organizations that align with those values.

49. We want to express ourselves artistically.

50. We want to explore and live out our spirituality.

51. We want to feel passionate about something.

52. We want a challenge.

53. We want to seek the truth.

Driving Force #5: Pleasure

54. We want to experience joy and happiness.

55. We want to experience sensual gratification.

56. We want instant gratification.

57. We want to experience stimulation and excitement.

58. We want to play.

59. We want to be loved.

Appendix B: Biases

The sixty or so biases described in this Appendix are organized into six classes as follows:

The first three of these classes are focused on us as <u>individuals</u>; the first is the class of biases that tend to be associated with when we are comparing ourselves, as individuals, with others. The second of these classes focuses on biases associated with the brain's reluctance to change. The final class regarding us as individuals is about biases concerned with how we are influenced in our thinking.

The final three classes address biases that are concerned with how we behave in <u>groups</u>. The first of these is how we think of ourselves as a group. Then we look at biases about how we regard other groups, or other people that are not in our group. The final class looks at biases about how we justify our behavior.

In each class, we have identified those one or two biases that we think have critical impact within that class.

Class 1 Biases:	Comparing ourselves as individuals to others
Critical Bias	Actor-Observer Bias
Additional Biases	Attentional bias, Egocentric bias, Empathy Gap, Extrinsic Incentives Bias, Hostile Attribution Bias, Illusion of Asymmetric Insight, Illusion of Transparency, Illusion of Validity, Illusory Superiority, Naïve Cynicism, Naïve Realism, Positivity Effect, Reactance, Restraint Bias, Righting Reflex, Self-serving Bias, Third-person Effect and Trait Ascription Bias.
Class 2 Biases:	Our reluctance to change as individuals
Critical Biases	Anchoring Effect Confirmation Bias
Additional Biases	Availability Cascade, Backfire Effect, Belief Bias, Conservatism Bias, Consistency Bias, Expectation Bias, Illusory Correlation, Observer-Expectancy Effect, and Status Quo Bias
Class 3 Biases:	Things that influence our individual thinking
Critical Biases	Illusion of Truth Effect Ladder of Inference
Additional Biases	Authority Bias, Defensive Attribution Hypothesis, Focusing Effect, Identifiable Victim Effect, Leveling and Sharpening, Mere Exposure Effect, Moral Credential Effect, Ostrich Effect, Persistence and Third-person Effect

Class 4 Biases:	How we view our group
Critical Biases	Bandwagon Effect: Ingroup bias
Additional Biases	Competitive Victimhood, Courtesy Bias, Cross-race Effect, Curse of Knowledge, False Consensus Effect, Group Attribution Error, Pluralistic ignorance, and Shared Information Bias
Class 5 Biases:	How we view other groups
Critical Biases	Ultimate Attribution Error:
Additional Biases	Just-World Hypothesis, Omission Bias, Outgroup Homogeneity Bias, Reactive Devaluation, Selective Perception, Stereotyping, and Zero-Sum Bias
Class 6 Biases:	How we justify what we do
Critical Biases	Framing Effect:
Additional Biases	Irrational Escalation

For each critical bias, we offer a formal definition, offer some expanded discussion, give some examples of where they occur, and give some typical statements that might result from such a bias. For the additional biases, which are relevant but maybe less important, we make it briefer; we give the formal name and the general description; for clarity in some cases we add a typical statement that illustrates the bias.

As you read through the list of biases, you might take a look and see which of them you recognize in yourself – or in others. It turns out that one of our biases, is that we notice other people's biases easier than we recognize our own.

Class 1: The Individual

These biases are associated with the process of comparing ourselves, as individuals, with other people. Many of these biases are oriented towards our own self-esteem; they provide a foundation for us to feel good about ourselves, and to feel superior to other people. We tend to believe that our actions are justified, that our opinions are grounded in fact, and that our decisions are not only fact based and rational but are fully thought through.

Actor-Observer Bias: We tend to explain other people's behavior by emphasizing their personality and de-emphasizing their situation. When we explain our own behavior, we let ourselves off the hook and tend to do the reverse. We blame our situation and de-emphasize our personality. *(You may hear this also as the Fundamental Attribution Error).*

The net effect of this is that we hold other people to different moral standards than we would hold ourselves even if we were in the same situation. In other words, we give ourselves an "out." We justify what <u>we</u> do as appropriate to the situation that we face, yet we blame <u>other people's</u> actions on their personalities. This bias is closely allied with the egocentric bias, explained below.

Here are a couple of ways that this bias plays itself out in every-day life.

- ➢ If someone else is late we reach a rapid conclusion that the person is unreliable. If we are late, even if it is by the same amount, or with the same frequency, we will offer traffic as an excuse.
- ➢ "It's important to make the distinction between passing on required information, which is what I do and being a gossip, which is what he does."

Attentional bias: We are affected by our recurring thoughts.

For many people, the continual process of thinking about what is happening in connection with race and associated issues, simply re-enforces their prior beliefs.

- ➢ "I have thought it over and over, and still end up where I started. It was the only thing I could have done."

Egocentric bias: Our tendency to explain personal success in terms of internal attributions and personal failure in terms of external attributions.

Frequently, we blame the situation when the expected results are negative, but we take credit for positive outcomes. This pattern of explaining outcomes tended to be reversed when evaluating others. For example, when failing an exam, we may think that it was much too difficult or that we were not feeling well, whereas the other students who failed did not learn enough.

Empathy Gap: We tend to underestimate the influence of our feelings or their strength. This is true both when we think about ourselves and when we think about others.

"What have black people got to complain about; they have equal rights. It's us that have lost our jobs."

Extrinsic Incentives Bias: This is when we see ourselves as having behavioral explanations (intrinsic) yet other people as having situational (extrinsic) explanations. It is an exception to the Actor-Observer Bias, and we use it when it serves us to do so.

"He just took the opportunity that presented itself, to be rude to the police officer. I would have held back."

Hostile Attribution Bias: We interpret the behavior of others as having hostile intent – even when we know little about them or the behavior could be viewed as ambiguous or benign. This is especially so when we are faced with strangers.

"Well, I thought he was about to take a swing at me. How did I know he was reaching for his glasses?"

Illusion of Asymmetric Insight: We believe that we know our peers better than they know us.

"Of course, I know how they think. They just never bother to find out what we think."

Illusion of Transparency: We overestimate the degree to which we know each other. We overestimate our ability to know other people, and we overestimate the degree to which they know us. *(An extension to the Illusion of Asymmetric Insight)*

"I know just how they think. They think we are bigoted and biased."

Illusion of Validity: We tend to have a belief that our judgements are accurate, and our decisions and recommendations are correct. This is especially the case when the available information is consistent.

This is best illustrated by a phrase that Phil tends to use: "Often wrong, never in doubt."

Illusory Superiority: When asked to describe ourselves, we all tend to overemphasize our perceived desirable qualities and underemphasize our undesirable qualities. *(Also known as Social Desirability Bias)*

"I always make rational decisions, and never let my emotions take over."

Naïve Cynicism: We have the belief that other people will have far more of an egocentric bias than we have.

"They always behave that way. All they ever think about is themselves."

Naïve Realism: We tend to believe that we have a lock on reality; that we alone are objective and unbiased, that the facts are clear, and that all rational people will agree with us. If you don't agree, then clearly you don't know the facts, are not thinking clearly or are just biased.

"If you think about it, there's only one conclusion to reach."

Positivity Effect: Older adults tend to focus on positive information in their memories, rather than negative. It's the origin of the "Glory Days."

"In our day, it was < *fill in the blank*>"

Reactance: Some of us have an urge to do the opposite of what someone else wants us to do. This is often seen as a perceived attempt to restrict your freedom of choice. It is most frequently seen manifested by people who score high in the need to be in control of their own destiny and/or to differentiate themselves from the group.

"I'm not just going to turn over and accept that … I am going to < *fill in the blank*> and I will show them."

Restraint Bias: We all have a tendency to overestimate our ability to show restraint in the face of temptation. This tendency can be exacerbated when we are in groups.

"I would have just let them get on with it. To each his own, I say."

Righting Reflex: [55] This involves the belief that you must convince or persuade (another) person to do the right thing. You just need to ask the right questions, find the proper arguments, give the critical information or pursue the correct logic to make the person see (reason) and change.

"Look I can explain to you exactly why that's the wrong approach to take."

Self-serving Bias: We have a tendency to evaluate ambiguous information in a way that is beneficial to our own beliefs or interests.

"I know that what he said could be taken in two ways, but it is obvious to me what he meant."

Trait Ascription Bias: We believe ourselves to be far more flexible in terms of personality, behavior and mood and see other people as predictable and rigid in their views.

"Oh, you know her. She's always that way."

Class 2: Reluctance to Change

The class of biases that are associated with the brain's reluctance to change. In the earlier section, we talked about the brain's reluctance to change i.e. to even entertain the integration of data which conflicts with what we think we already know. This series of biases start to explain some of the reasons for this. In addition, our brain feels rewarded when we act consistently from one day to the next. It gives us a better sense of prediction.

In many ways, the next two biases can be considered the "mothers-of-all-biases" in that they are both so widespread.

Anchoring Effect: We have a tendency to rely too heavily, or "anchor," on one trait or piece of information when making decisions (usually the first piece of information acquired on that subject). This anchoring effect is extremely widespread and arises in many instances where you would least expect it.

An 'anchor' in the brain can be placed in a number of ways, often by words, questions, numbers or graphics. The really sad and insidious aspects of this bias are that we often don't know it has been placed in our brains. The impact of anchoring has been measured in a broad array of different domains, such as price estimates, estimates of self-efficacy, probability assessments, legal judgments, negotiations and many others.

Also, the impact of the anchoring influence can be drastic and unconnected with the subject at hand. In a famous experiment the price that someone was willing to pay for an item in an auction was influenced by the last two digits of a social security number.

In another series of experiments in wine and liquor stores, it was found that the music played influenced people's buying decisions. French music playing influenced people to buy more French wines.

"Oh yes, I know all about that. I heard a great article on CNN a couple of years back."

Confirmation Bias: We have a tendency to search for, interpret, focus on, and remember information in a way that confirms our preconceptions. It doesn't matter what your background, religious or political leanings, without explicitly deciding to do otherwise, most of us tend to hang out in those spaces which confirm and support out beliefs. It's like a warm, cozy blanket. The brain doesn't have to think hard.

The impact? If you listen to CNN, then you will probably always listen to CNN; if you listen to Fox News, likewise.

In addition, the more confident we feel about our position or a belief that we hold, the more this bias is likely to show up.

Furthermore, as we listen to other people's positions and belief's, our brains fail to even recognize the strength of others' disconfirming opinions to alter our own, yet we recognize and take those strengths into account when their opinions confirm our own. Research has been shown that, deep within our brains, there is reduced neural sensitivity to the strength of others' opinions when their opinions are disconfirming. Our existing judgments alter the neural representation of new information strength, leaving us less likely to alter opinions in the face of disagreement. [56]

"See what I mean? That just shows I have been right all along. They are just that way."

Availability Cascade: A self-reinforcing process in which a collective belief gains more and more plausibility through its increasing repetition in public discourse. Repeat something long enough and often enough and it will become true.

Statements about any particular group, if repeated often enough, will start to take root and be believed by an ever-widening population. This approach is often used in political campaigns.

Backfire Effect: Some people's reaction to disconfirming evidence is simply to double down on their previous beliefs. Regardless of the apparent truth of new data being presented, people who already hold strong beliefs will not be persuaded by new information or logic. In fact, the process of trying to change their mind, may make matters worse.

"I hear what you are saying, but it doesn't change my opinion one iota."

Belief Bias: An effect where someone's evaluation of the logical strength of an argument is biased by the believability of the conclusion. If we believe something to be true, then we will evaluate the information presented to us with the conclusion already in mind.

"You make a good point, but that is what I have said all along."

Conservatism Bias: The tendency to revise one's belief insufficiently when presented with new evidence. *(Also known as Continued Influence Effect; see also Backfire effect)*

"I know that is new data, but I don't think it is relevant to this discussion."

Consistency Bias: This manifests itself in two ways. First, we incorrectly remember our past attitudes and behavior as resembling our present attitudes and behavior. Second, our brain's love consistency, so we will tend to act in line with how we have always acted. It feels safer that way.

"I know I have always thought that."

Expectation Bias: The tendency for experts to believe, certify, and publish data that agree with their expectations and to disbelieve, discard, or downgrade the corresponding weightings for data that appear to conflict with those expectations.

"These data just confirm what I have been saying all along."

Illusory Correlation: The tendency to inaccurately perceive a relationship between two unrelated events.

According to Jason, this happens to minorities all the time; "They laid me off today…must be because I'm black" despite the fact that the company went bankrupt.

Observer-Expectancy Effect: When we expect someone to behave a certain way, we will interpret what we see to support what we expected to see – even when the data doesn't necessarily support it.

"I told you that's what would happen."

Status Quo Bias: The tendency to like things to stay relatively the same. Existing social, economic, and political arrangements tend to be preferred and alternatives disparaged, sometimes even at the expense of individual and collective self-interest. *(Also known as System Justification.)*

"Let's not change anything right now; rather let's wait and see what happens."

Class 3: The way we are influenced

The class of biases, that addresses biases, that explain how we are influenced in our thinking. Our brains are influenced by many things. Some influences are general in that they seem to apply to many people across many cultures; these are such things as authority figures, scarcity, other people's opinions, and the need to return a favor. Others are more oriented towards our individual experiences and background.

Illusion of Truth Effect: People are more likely to identify as true, those statements that they have previously heard (even if they cannot consciously remember having heard them), regardless of the actual validity of the statement. In other words, a person is more likely to believe a familiar statement than an unfamiliar one. Even drastic untruths can enter our common knowledge base, by the use of repetition.

We would also hope that if we are forearmed with knowledge, then we won't be influenced by untruthful repetition. Unfortunately, it turns out that that is not the case. Inside the brain, repeated statements are easier to process, and subsequently perceived to be more truthful, than new statements, even if we have knowledge that support the new statements. [57]

The danger with untruthful or unvalidated statements being repeated, is that the listener tends only to hear the allegation, and not any of the caveats and qualifications that might follow the statements – like, this news has not been validated. This gets to be even more insidious if the news is being reported by a trustworthy, reputable news source as if it were fact.

And surely, if the statements themselves or the information contained therein, are implausible or preposterous, our brains will not be so influenced? Once again, this is not the case. We are still taken in. Fazio et all summarize it this way:

> *"Our results indicate that the illusory truth effect is highly robust and occurs across all levels of plausibility. Therefore, even highly implausible statements will become more plausible with enough repetition."* [58]

Scary huh?

"It's all over social media. Everyone is talking about it therefore, I know it seems crazy, but it must be true."

Authority Bias: The tendency to attribute greater accuracy to the opinion of an authority figure (unrelated to its content) and be more influenced by that opinion. As we watch and listen to news, the very fact that there is a personality who is delivering that news or opinion, influences the degree to which we are swayed by what we hear. In many cases, the higher "up the ladder" the deliverer is, the more influence they have over our opinion. In addition, if the deliverer is labeled as an expert, or is wearing a symbol of authority (e.g. a uniform or a white coat) we tend to be even more influenced by what they are saying.

"But that's what Doctor *<fill in the blank>* said, and after all, she should know."

Defensive Attribution Hypothesis: Attributing more blame to a harm-doer as the outcome becomes more severe or as our personal or situational similarity to the victim increases.

"Wow. I realize that that could have been me."

Focusing Effect: The tendency to place too much importance on one aspect of an event.

"Someone got shot in Seattle, showing that every one of the protesters are there to loot, promote anarchy, and commit acts of violence."

Identifiable Victim Effect: The tendency to respond more strongly to a single identified person at risk than to a large group of people at risk.

"What happened to her was awful."

Leveling and Sharpening: Memory distortions introduced by the loss of details in a recollection over time, often concurrent with sharpening or selective recollection of certain details that take on exaggerated significance in relation to the details or aspects of the experience lost through leveling. Both biases may be reinforced over time and by repeated recollection or retelling of a memory.

"All I remember is that it was just wrong. Plain wrong."

Mere Exposure Effect: Our tendency to express undue liking for things merely because of familiarity with them.

This often manifests itself when considering filling a job role. We will eliminate the internal candidate … because we know their faults, and take a risk with an external candidate, about whom we know nothing.

Moral Credential Effect: The tendency of a track record of non-prejudice to increase subsequent prejudice.

"Just take a look at my past voting record. It shows I am not prejudiced."

Ostrich Effect: Our tendency to ignore an obvious (negative) situation.

"It does not impact me; all the violence is in crime-ridden slums."

Persistence: The unwanted recurrence of memories of a traumatic event

We replay events over and over again in our mind and ruminate on them, which re-enforces them in our brains.

Third-person Effect: We have a belief that mass communicated media messages have a greater effect on others than on ourselves.

"It's easy for me to detect fake news. I am not taken in by it at all."

Class 4: How we see our group

The class of biases that offer an explanation about how we see 'our group' and members of our group. Most of us like to be with people that we like and that are just like us. Our ingroup! It makes us feel comfortable and safe. We nonconsciously assign (positive) characteristics to our ingroup and tend to contrast those characteristics with those who are not in our ingroup. We treat the people in our in-group differently than we treat those who are not.

We form ingroups, often without knowing it, in a very short time. Whereas it used to be that ingroups were primarily geographically based, social media has made it easier to rapidly form ingroups in many locations

If the Anchoring effect and Confirmation bias are the mothers-of-all-biases, the next two biases have to be right up there with them in their ubiquity.

Bandwagon Effect: Our tendency to do (or believe) things because many other people do (or believe) the same. Related to groupthink and herd behavior. We are all influenced by what other people think. It is very difficult to hold beliefs that differ from one's own group – and even more difficult to express them in public.

The bandwagon effect has impact on everything between voting and buying luxury goods, and there is a vast amount of research on all aspects of the effect. Most of the research suggests that we are all susceptible to the opinions of other people; in the age of social media many web-sites have made effective use of this effect, FaceBook "likes" (in helping people form opinions) and Yelp (in making purchase choices or attendance selections) being two prime examples.

The research clearly shows a bandwagon effect in polling and subsequent voting choices; the resulting impact, however, is less than clear. On the one hand, the tendency for people to want to vote with the winner, will give an advantage to the leading candidate in a poll. On the other hand, the tendency for some people to want to vote for the underdog, will give the training candidate an advantage. In either case, however, people tend to be swayed by how other people will vote – or at least say how they intend to vote!

Where this effect gets to be worrisome is when it is combined with, for example, the Illusion of Truth Effect; we can become influenced by the stated beliefs of others, even though how they reached those beliefs may simply be based upon the repetition of untruths.

"Just ask anyone here, everyone feels the same way about what's going on."

"I just spoke with my neighbor and she said that the social media feeds are full of people wanting to be part of the movement."

Ingroup bias: The tendency for people to give preferential treatment to others they perceive to be members of their own groups.

The APA [u] definition is as follows: [59]

> *"The tendency to favor one's own group, its members, its characteristics, and its products, particularly in reference to other groups. The favoring of the **ingroup** tends to be more pronounced than the rejection of the outgroup, but both tendencies become more pronounced during periods of intergroup contact."*

This bias has impact in a wide variety of situations, probably too numerous to address here. In relation to the subject of this book, it is easy to see that we need to understand the impact that ingroup bias has on racial and ethnic minorities in, at least, the following spaces: the public at large, on police treatment and the judicial process. For the sake of brevity, we are choosing to ignore the many other areas where ingroup bias shows up, for example, sports teams and violence, medical diagnosis and treatment of racial and ethnic minorities and the political impacts of racism and discrimination.

One author gives us some good descriptions of the impacts of ingroup bias, as follows:

> " ... *experiments have shown that when subjects are matched with others who are labeled as members of an ingroup, they are more likely to reward those ingroup members for good behavior, ... that the ingroup effect is stronger when ingroup members have social ties (as opposed to just having been labeled as belonging to the same group), and that there is evidence for the existence of heightened empathy toward ingroup members."*

One recent hypothesis for ingroup bias is that from an evolutionary point of view, ingroup bias reduced uncertainty and hence increased survival possibilities. Another body of research in support of ingroup bias being evolutionary advantageous suggests that there is " ... *consistent*

---

u APA = American Psychological Association

evidence for increased neural responses to the perceived pain of same-race compared with other-race individuals in multiple brain regions and across multiple time-windows."

To be clear, all of us belong to a multitude of ingroups, and those ingroups can be formed very quickly, even within minutes. Gender, ethnicity, occupation, economic, social position, hobbies, pet ownership – have all become the basis for ingroups to form. There is nothing wrong with being in an ingroup, per se.

There are, however, a couple of downsides which may not be immediately obvious; first, an ingroup can feel exclusive to anyone looking at it from the outside – i.e. to members of the outgroup. That exclusion can give a sense of rejection or disenfranchisement just by the fact of not being part of the group. That is bad enough, but then the second downside comes into play. Members of an ingroup can feel and demonstrate a sense of superiority to members of the outgroup – and this is often the beginning of prejudice.

"I don't want my children going to a mixed-race school."

Competitive Victimhood: Groups that perceive themselves as victims can engage in "competitive victimhood". In some societal circumstances, this competition bears on the recognition of past sufferings, rather than on their relative severity, fostering negative intergroup attitudes.

"They don't have it nearly as bad as we do."

Courtesy Bias: Our tendency to give an opinion that is more socially correct than one's true opinion so as to avoid offending anyone.

"I know what he said was wrong, but I didn't speak up because it was not the right time and place for me to do so. It would have made a scene."

Cross-race Effect: The tendency for people of one race to have difficulty identifying members of a race other than their own.

This is widespread across all races – most white people can't tell black people apart. Or Asians. And many black people cannot tell white people apart. The impact is huge in terms of the accuracy of witness testimony, which is poor at the best of times.

"They all look the same to me."

Curse of Knowledge: When better-informed people find it extremely difficult to think about problems from the perspective of lesser-informed people.

"How could they (white people) not have known racism was still a thing?"

False Consensus Effect: The tendency for people to overestimate the degree to which others agree with them.

"Well, I think we are in agreement that this is our approach, so I don't think we need more discussion."

Group Attribution Error: The biased belief that the characteristics of an individual group member are reflective of the group as a whole, or the tendency to assume that group decision outcomes reflect the preferences of group members, even when information is available that clearly suggests otherwise.

There is nothing wrong with "attribution." We all do it, all of the time. It is the process we use to try to understand and explain the behavior of others; why they have acted as they did in a given situation and what the causes were for that behavior." It is when we are wrong in our attribution that we get into trouble. We are especially susceptible to being wrong, perceiving the observed behavior actions as negative.

"I don't know why black people are upset about police when they are all shooting each other in inner cities."

"We shouldn't have a female American President because other countries will think we're weak being led by a female" [v]

Pluralistic ignorance: Misperception of a group norm, that results from observing people who are acting at variance with their private beliefs, out of a concern for the social consequences; those actions reinforce the erroneous group norm.

Pluralistic ignorance describes the case in which virtually every member of a group or society privately rejects a belief, opinion, or practice, yet believes that virtually every other member privately accepts it. The term "pluralistic ignorance" is something of a misnomer, for in these cases, group members are not, in fact, ignorant of one another's private sentiments; rather, they think they know, but are mistaken.

---

[v] Actual statement reported to one of the authors.

Shared Information Bias: The tendency for group members to spend more time and energy discussing information that all members are already familiar with (i.e., shared information) and less time and energy discussing information that only some members are aware of (i.e., unshared information). If this is combined with ingroup bias, confirmation bias, courtesy bias, and our tendency to reject new information which flies in the face of pre-existing notions, we can start to see why getting a group to change their mind is very difficult

If you want some great examples of how this is driven or manifests, just spend a few minutes on cable news. Fox will spend a lot of time on an issue that CNN will ignore, and vice versa.

Class 5: How we view other groups

This class covers those biases that explain how we view and think about those people that are not part of our group. Once we have formed an ingroup, the group tends to develop a set of "shared" opinions about people who are not part of the ingroup. The group tends to simplify the view it has of others and lump every individual member of the outgroup as having the same characteristics. In some cases, the members of the ingroup privately might disagree with the "shared" opinions of the group, but often will not speak up and won't rock the boat.

Ultimate Attribution Error: The tendency for persons from one group (the ingroup) to determine that any bad acts by members of an outgroup are caused by internal attributes or traits rather than by outside circumstances or situations, while viewing their positive behaviors as merely exceptions to the rule or the result of luck. Conversely, ingroup members will overestimate the effects of their own perceived internal attributes and underplay situational forces when evaluating their successes, and they will place more emphasis on external factors when explaining their failures or faults.

Thomas Pettigrew originated the term in 1979 and explained it as follows: Ultimate attribution error occurs when ingroup members (1) attribute negative outgroup behavior to internal factors (more than they would for identical ingroup behavior), and (2) attribute positive outgroup behavior to one or more of the following causes: (a) a fluke or exceptional case, (b) luck or special advantage, (c) high motivation and effort, and (d) external situational factors.

This is where we really start to get into trouble.

> *"This attributional double standard makes it virtually impossible for outgroup members to break free of prejudice against them, because their positive actions are explained away while their failures and shortcomings are used against them."* [60]

Let's look at three studies illustrating this bias:

One study found that white students were more likely to interpret a shove as violent -- and more likely to explain it dispositionally -- when the shove came from a black person than a white person.

Another study found that Hindu participants were more likely to make dispositional attributions for negative behaviors than positive behaviors when the actor was Muslim but showed the opposite pattern when the actor was Hindu.

And a review of 58 different experiments found that on traditionally masculine tasks, male successes were more likely than female successes to be attributed to ability, whereas male failures were more likely than female failures to be attributed to bad luck or lack of effort.

In other words, we give our ingroup a break and we don't give a break to the outgroup!

"If blacks are so worried about police violence, why do they all keep killing each other in inner cities?"

Just-World Hypothesis: The tendency for people to want to believe that the world is fundamentally just, causing them to rationalize an otherwise inexplicable injustice as deserved by the victim(s).

"Well, it's clear to me that they were just asking for trouble."

Omission Bias: The tendency to judge harmful actions as worse, or less moral, than equally harmful omissions (inactions).

'We don't need to change police training or change attitudes we just need people to stop looting and desecrating monuments."

Outgroup Homogeneity Bias: The tendency whereby we see members of our own group as being relatively more varied than members of other groups.

"Clearly we have a wider handle on the issue than they do."

Reactive Devaluation: The tendency whereby we devalue proposals only because they purportedly originated with an adversary. *(Also manifests as the not-invented-here syndrome)*

"Look at who proposed that amendment. Of course, they would think that."

Selective Perception: The tendency for expectations to affect perception.

This applies across the board, whether it is one race thinking about another, or a teacher being told that one group of students is not quite as bright as the others. *(Also known as the Pygmalion Effect)*

If you have poor expectations of < fill-in-the-blank> then you will perceive everything they do as not good enough.

Stereotyping: Expecting a member of a group to have certain characteristics, and acting accordingly, without having actual information about that individual.

"Well. What do you expect? They are all like that."

Zero-Sum Bias: A bias whereby a situation is incorrectly perceived to be like a zero-sum game (i.e., one person gains at the expense of another).

"If that happens, then they'll take all our jobs."

Class 6: Some ways we justify our actions

The class of biases that looks at biases regarding how we justify our behavior. The brain is really good at making things up. We take our nonconscious decisions, choices and actions and use the rational part of our brain to come up with a plausible narrative. We develop explanations for our actions, often simply to justify them to other ingroup members.

Framing Effect: A bias whereby we draw different, and possibly opposite, conclusions from the same information, depending on how that information is presented and anchored.

Digging slightly deeper, it is when we are faced with two choices that are "logically equivalent" but, at first glance, do not appear to be the same. Typically, each choice highlights either a positive or a negative attribute relating to the choice.

Let's look at a couple of examples:

"This policy would result in 10% unemployment" vs "This policy will ensure 90% employment."

"The Covid-19 pandemic is likely to mean that 2% of those infected will die" vs "The good news is that 98% of people are likely to survive Covid-19."

Druckman [61] explains it to us nicely:

> *"Specifically, a framing effect is said to occur when, in the course of describing an issue or event, a speaker's emphasis on a subset of potentially relevant considerations causes individuals to focus on these considerations when constructing their opinions."*

The Framing Effect is so powerful, that it is deliberately and frequently used in Advertising and Politics. Indeed, it is so powerful in politics that some countries banned political advertising in the final days before an election.

Irrational Escalation: The phenomenon where people justify increased investment in a decision based on the cumulative prior investment, despite new evidence suggesting that the decision was probably wrong. *(Also known as the sunk cost fallacy.)*

"We don't need to change police training. We just need more of them to crack down harder on protesters, like they have been doing."

Appendix C: Change readiness

The Stages

1. **Pre-contemplation:** This is the stage in which an individual or group has no intention to change behavior in the foreseeable future. People in precontemplation do not see their behaviors as a problem and therefore see no need to change. This is sometimes called the "ignorance is bliss" stage. People in the precontemplation stage have traditionally been thought of as "resistant to change." Unfortunately, if someone doesn't see their behaviors as a problem and are not interested in changing, we still need to know how to work with them. Although many people in precontemplation might, by definition, never be available for the type of change we are considering. Note that some people in this category include anyone who has been pressured or coerced into attending one of our classes or other interventions.

   It is possible that the people in this category have, in the past, thought about trying to change their behaviors but, for a variety of reasons, were unsuccessful. Because the change didn't work or didn't stick, or they experienced some kind of negative reaction within their ingroup, they now see change as not worth pursuing.

2. **Contemplation:** In this stage, people recognize a problem and are contemplating a change, but haven't yet committed to changing. People in contemplation are sitting on the fence – part of them wants to change, but an equally compelling part of them wants to stay the same. The stage in which people are aware that they need action, and/or are seriously thinking about doing something about it but have not yet made a commitment to take action. People at this stage struggle between their positive evaluations of changing their behavior versus the amount of effort, energy, and loss it will cost to overcome and solidify the change.

   This stage is all about ambivalence. People can stay in contemplation for a very long time. Change is tough. It is hard to take that first step. Chronic contemplators spend lots of time thinking and not much time doing. This is in part because "contemplators struggle to understand their problem, to see its causes, and to think about possible solutions"

   In the case of racism, they may be hearing a lot about it, but have yet, for example, to get off the fence as to whether they even support Black Lives Matter.

3. **Preparation:** This is the stage in which individuals are intending to take action within the foreseeable future, say one month. They are considering some small behavioral changes

("baby steps") - they are "testing the waters.". They may be catching themselves behaving or thinking in a certain way that now makes them feel uncomfortable.

Those little steps might have failed to produce any significant change, or they might have worked, but they have not resulted in the kind of behavior change that moves them forward. They recognize the issue, might want to change, have had some occasions over the recent past where they have done something differently but are mostly engaged in the old behaviors, even though they don't necessarily want to.

4.   **Action:** The stage in which individuals modify their thinking, behavior, experiences, and/or environment to address the change that they are wishing to make. Action involves the most overt behavioral changes and requires considerable commitment of both time and energy.

5.   **Maintenance:** The stage in which people work to prevent relapse and consolidate the gains attained during action. This stage extends from 6 months to an indeterminate period past the initial action.

6.   **Relapse:** When people are attempting to change long-standing habits and replace them with new ones, it can sometimes take a while, and some backsliding does occur. Recognizing and talking about the possibility of a relapse upfront, can take the guilt and sting out of such an event, and promote the longer-term overall change. They are not the first person to slip-up and make a mistake.

Questions to determine readiness

Precontemplation: Some questions to ask or assessments to make:

"With regard to racism, Black Lives Matter or discrimination in general, have you considered making any changes to your thinking, behavior or actions in the next six months."

To what extent do you agree with the following statements:

"I guess I have faults, but there's nothing that I really need to change"
"As far as I'm concerned, I don't have any problems that need changing"
"I know I am not perfect, but I'm no worse than anyone else that I know, so why should I change?"

If you hear something to the effect:

"Yeah, I'm not perfect, but I'm so much better than I used to be and I'm really trying hard not to fall back into my old ways of behaving"

then this person has attempted to change and has failed. They may actually be in a "maintenance" stage.

There are two stages in which someone doesn't see a problem: precontemplation, or maintenance. In all the other stages, contemplation, preparation, action and relapse, the person sees a problem.

What you might consider: We have to tailor any action to match the person's stage of change. For people in precontemplation, research has found that it can be helpful to increase awareness about the problem. This can be done in a number of ways. The very act of interviewing, carrying out a survey or doing an assessment, can be the first step in raising awareness.

We have to work on both the emotional brain and the logical brain. You will hear that mantra for interventions at all stages.

Here is an example intervention designed to move people emotionally. Present a direct testimony from someone who has experienced racism or show videos of racist actions. Follow this with an assignment and ask attendees to write about the abuse, discrimination or racism from the recipient's perspective.

And on the logical side:

Have a session where the attendees discuss the benefits of changing

Have a session to encourage the individual to look at the consequences of what is happening now

Have attendees write down discrepancies between the way the individual is, where society would like them to be and where they would like to be.

Contemplation: You can assess for contemplation by listening for statements like:

"I know I have a problem, but I'm not really sure I want to do anything about it."

"I'm not really sure what I can do about it."

"I know that a lot of people say I should change, but I'm not really sure how."

Once again, a reminder: we have to work on both the emotional brain and the logical brain.

The most important thing to remember about an exchange with someone in contemplation is that they are evaluating the pros and cons of change but haven't yet decided to change. If you start making suggestions about what they "should" change or do, or how to change, the part of the person that wants things to stay the same will bring up all of the reasons why change is not possible. The last thing you want to do is have them talk themselves into not changing their thoughts, statements and behaviors. In addition, "shoulds" and suggestions can often feel like being told what to do, rather than being allowed to make up our own minds and have freedom of choice.

We all have a tendency to want to "tell someone the solution to everything that they are doing wrong or that ails them." The average person does not like to be told what to do – especially if that implies that they have been doing things wrong in the past. The brain hates to think that it was wrong.

Spend more time asking them what they think their approach could be. From the brain's perspective, if they come up with an "aha" or an idea, no matter how simple, then there is a greater chance of them actually acting on it, than if you suggest something.

Interventions structured around them developing ideas, either as individuals or in groups of two or three, are more likely to effect change than a list delivered in written, electronic or lecture format. These could be done in a number of ways:

"What are the pros and cons of changing?" – Logical brain appeal
"What are the downsides of staying the same?" - Logical brain appeal
"What are the best outcomes for you if you were to change? – some emotional appeal

Another way to approach this is by providing the person with education about how things could be, such as books or videos that illustrate new behaviors. This kind of information is useless in

Precontemplation because people don't see a problem, but it works well in contemplation because they've partially bought into the idea that they want to change but are not sure how.

Some people who even have an inkling about changing behavior can be fearful almost to the point of paralysis. They need hope, support and a sense that they can get there. They need to overcome the resistance ... and all of those things keeping them where they are.

Develop a set of questions based on where they are with regard to class 2 biases – i.e. biases that tend to make us want to stay the same. Discuss with them or have small group discussions.

Preparation: You want to listen for statements like:

"I really want to change because..."

"I wish I could just figure out how to..."

Ask questions like:

"What questions do you have about how to think and behave differently?"

"If you don't change, how will you ever be the person you want to be."

"What have you already tried doing? To what extent were you successful?"

"Where have you made changes before?

"How did you go about doing that?"

If you have the opportunity of a conversation with the person preparing to change, assist them in defining a number of things:

- How they would think, act and behave in their new self?
- What their first steps might be?
- To what degree do they think they are able to achieve the change?
- How will they know if they have been successful?
- What support systems do they have?
- What new knowledge will they need?
- What new skills might they want to acquire?
- What help might they need from you?
- How will they respond to the inevitable challenges that come from their friends and family?
- How can they ensure that the steps they take are small and achievable in a short period of time?

Remember, at this stage, they are planning to change – they haven't actually taken a step in the direction of change – and they are still entertaining all sorts of internal questions.

Action: People in the action phase have started to put into practice the plan they developed in the preparation phase. Maybe they are consciously experimenting choosing new behaviors, being confronted with challenges to the new behaviors, and consequently gaining new insight and developing new skills.

If they have had some small success, people in the Action stage can become enthusiastic and motivated.

Listen for statements that indicate both an acknowledgement of a prior problem and new behaviors.

Provide verbal reinforcement and support the person's belief that he or she can sustain the change.

If you are able to, identify specific behaviors that the person has changed and connect them with the goals (or changes of behavior) that they had previously set for themselves. Congratulate them in having the courage to take the steps they have and encourage them to celebrate in some small way.

Maintenance: In this stage, people have been engaged in the new behavior for at least six months and are committed to maintaining the new behavior.

What you are looking for here is when the person reports actions they have taken, how they dealt with the results and a description of how that differs from their prior behavior.

Additional conversations might revolve around how your client is sustaining their commitment to the new behavior. You could talk about what could go wrong … and help them develop a number of things that they could do to prevent that from happening, what they would do if they caught themselves, and what they would do to recover.

Look out for the person who, having had a couple of successes, might become overconfident and stretch themselves too far.

Help them develop strategies for what to do if they do stretch too far, or relapse into old behaviors.

Appendix D: Problem Types

Texts on problem solving & decision making, tend to lump all problems into one big bucket and then take a one-size-fits-all approach to the issue. The sense of many researchers is that this is a mistake. Problems tend to fall into three big buckets, each of which requires a different approach. For the sake of this Appendix, we will refer to them as Critical, Clock and Cloud. [w] It is the "Cloud" ones that are the challenge and where we will focus our explanations, but for the sake of completeness we will briefly explain the others:

Critical problems: As the title implies, these tend to have the characteristics of being urgent, require immediate attention and, sometimes, extremely difficult. In general, with critical problems, getting committees and focus groups together is NOT the solution. The approach needs to be command and control, hopefully led by someone who has seen the issue or something like it before. Examples might be, as is the case while writing this book, massive fires in California, or the server has been hacked.

Afterwards you might do a review (sometimes called a post-mortem or mop-up) to learn what you might do differently next time.

Clock problems: These are regular day-to-day problems that we face all the time. These tend to be mechanical, finite, predictable and, relatively, controllable. They range from simple to complex. The common theme behind these is the need for resource – time, money, expertise, effective teams etc. – in order to solve them.

At the simple end of the scale are problems like, what kind of car should I buy next, how do I build an extension to the back of my house, or what should we have for dinner? Sometimes they are solved by one person, but frequently they require a small group of people to get together, agree upon a goal, agree a process and plan the solution. You know that there is a solution, and you just have to find the optimum one, given your resource restraints. There are many problem-solving approaches – a quick Internet search will give you plenty. But they all involve goals and planning.

At the other end of the scale are the complex problems, which can be somewhat more challenging. They are complex for a number of reasons; the complexity can come from the difficulty of the problem itself or the difficulty of the solution, or some mixture of both. Sending a man to the moon by the end of the decade is one such a problem. Delivering people and resources to the International Space Station is another example. But the fundamental approach

---

[w] An adaptation of Karl Popper's nomenclature

is the same as for simple problems. Develop a plan and proceed according to the plan, once again taking into account your resource constraints. Again, they all involve goals and planning, although involving larger numbers of resources than simple problems.

Cloud Problems: Without taking the title too far as a metaphor, they range from fluffy clouds, which are difficult to understand but have minimal scope, to storm clouds that have major impact and can have serious consequences if not solved. These latter are also known as wicked problems.

Wicked problems. These are a whole different kettle of fish. They are variously described in books, but typically the description goes something like this:

> *A wicked problem is a social or cultural problem that is difficult or impossible to solve for as many as four reasons: incomplete or contradictory knowledge, the number of people or opinions involved, the large economic burden, and the interconnected nature of these problems with other problems."* [62]

Do some of the elements of this ring a bell with, racism, the topic at hand? Let's dig further using the same website:

> *"These problems are typically offloaded to policy makers or are written off as being too cumbersome to handle en masse. Yet these are the problems—poverty, sustainability, equality, and health and wellness—that plague our cities and our world and that touch each and every one of us."*

Wicked problems are not just complex problems with a higher degree of complexity. They require a fundamentally different approach to problem solving. Traditional, linear-based, problem solving mechanisms won't get you to the solution – if there even is one! The approach of setting goals and planning how to achieve those goals simply don't work for this type of problem.

In some cases, compounding the problem solution is that *"the conditions and constraints affecting the problem and its possible solutions change over time, sometimes dramatically and rapidly, - changing both the problem and the range of options to address it."* Sometimes, in attempting to address it, the act of attempting to solve the problem can actually make matters worse!

Experts in the field of wicked problems suggest that there are some basic characteristics:

➢ It is difficult, or maybe impossible, to define them.
➢ The same problem may manifest itself differently in different areas

- It is not clear about who "owns" the problem
- It is hard, or maybe impossible, to measure or claim success because they are typically linked to many other problems
- There may not be an "end-state goal"
- A solution may not exist.
- Solutions might only be measured in terms of better or worse
- Solutions need to be highly flexible and adaptable – steps taken to improve the situation rather than completely solve it.
- There are rarely templates to follow; other similar situations might provide some guides, but small differences can make drastic impacts on the approach taken.
- Teams that tackle wicked problems have to be good at making things up as they go along
- There is always more than one explanation for the cause of a wicked problem; the appropriateness of the explanation will depend upon the viewpoint of the explainer.
- There are always many stakeholders involved, all of which has a different interest and a different recommended solution.
- A wicked problem is very often a symptom of another wicked problem.
- You may never know whether you got it right. Maybe another solution would have produced a better outcome.
- There is rarely an opportunity for trial and error approaches
- Every wicked problem is unique
- Taking a step to resolving a wicked problem may make the problem worse.
- Teams that tackle wicked problems need to be held responsible for their actions.
- Solutions to wicked problems inevitably involve the involvement and support of multiple, if not all, stakeholders.
- It may be difficult, at least at first, to identify all of the stakeholders, and get them engaged. Sometimes, additional stakeholders come out of the woodwork at a later stage.
- Solutions inevitably involve a high degree of persistence.

To be a wicked problem, the problem does not have to have all of those characteristics; just having several of them will qualify!

Almost by definition, then, the issue of racism and discrimination comes clearly under the category of a wicked problem.

Traditional problem-solving approaches have often been focused on defining success, planning, and speed to solution. The solution to wicked problems involves bringing in multiple perspectives with wide-ranging knowledge, a high degree of willingness to collaborate, a great ability to facilitate difficult discussions, open minds and perseverance.

Appendix E. Increasing courage

The purpose of this appendix is to expand upon the aspects of courageously competent people that we outlined in the section on other influences on the brain.

In a recent HBR article, [63] Detert gave us a brief list of activities that courageously competent people carry out or the conditions they create and/or ensure are in place. These are:

> - Laying the groundwork - by establishing a strong internal reputation
> - Improving their fallback options in case things go poorly
> - Carefully choosing their battles
> - Discerning whether a given opportunity to act makes sense in light of their values, the timing, and their broader objectives
> - Maximizing the odds of in-the-moment success by managing the messaging and emotions
> - Following up to preserve relationships and marshal commitment

Laying the groundwork:
- by establishing a strong internal reputation
- being seen as invested in the success of the organization
- playing things even handedly
- accumulating a stock of goodwill and trust from other stakeholders
- engaging with, listening to, and empathizing with other people
- helping other people develop

Carefully choosing their battles:
- discerning whether a given opportunity to act makes sense in light of their values, the timing, and their broader objectives
- performing a risk-reward assessment (See Chapter 8 on Decision making)
- obtaining a good answer to the "Why this? Why now?" questions
- being aware of personal emotional triggers, biases and patterns
- being aware of other people's emotional triggers, biases and patterns
- balancing short term wins with competing longer-term wins

- being acutely aware of timing and what else is going on
- acting when potential support is above a minimal threshold

Maximizing the odds of in-the-moment success by managing the messaging and emotions:
- focusing on framing the issue in terms that the audience will relate to (remember, the brain is strongly influenced by framing)
- making effective use of data, information and knowledge that is available
- managing the emotions in the room – your own and others
- connecting their agenda to the organization's priorities, values, direction and culture
- explaining how your idea addresses critical areas of concern for all stakeholders.
- ensuring that other decision makers feel included—not attacked or pushed aside
- divide and conquer – work one on one beforehand to get some support in the room

Following up to preserve relationships and marshal commitment.
- following up after they take action, no matter how things turned out
- thanking supporters and sharing credit.
- addressing lingering emotions
- repairing relationships with those who might be hurt or angry.
- taking a one-size-fits-one approach to each stakeholder
- recognizing that every stakeholder has a different Personal Threat Profile

Other aspects that are paramount:
- tackling small issues in order to practice and gain experience
- imagining – imagining yourself in a given situation and how you would ideally respond; this gives the brain the sense that "we've been here before" when a real-life situation arrives
- explore the boundaries: what's the best-case outcome? What's the worst? Do I have plans to take the next steps in either case?

- recognizing that courage is not a 'stand-alone' attribute – it is highly related to who you are, what you stand for, how you make decisions, your tolerance for risk-taking, your tolerance for ambiguity …. and many other facets.

Appendix F: Reading, Viewing and Listening

Recommended Books, Books for Teens & Children, Movies, Podcasts and Comic Books or Graphic Novels on Race, Class and Social Justice

Books	
Author	**Title**
Alexander, Michelle	*The New Jim Crow: Mass Incarceration in the Age of Colorblindness*
Channing Brown, Austin	*I'm Still Here: Black Dignity in a World Made for Whiteness*
Gottschalk, Marie	*Caught: The Prison State and the Lockdown of American Politics*
Coates, Ta-Nehisi	*Between the World and Me*
Coates, Ta-Nehisi	*We Were Eight Years in Power*
Coates, Ta-Nehisi	*The Beautiful Struggle A Father, Two Sons, and an Unlikely Road to Manhood*
Eddo-Lodge, Reni	*Why I'm No Longer Talking to White People About Race*
Fleming, Crystal	*How to Be Less Stupid About Race: On Racism, White Supremacy, and the Racial Divide*
Fredrickson, George	*Racism: A Short History*
Haley, Alex	*The Autobiography of Malcolm X*
Harvey, Jennifer	*Raising White Kids: Bringing Up Children in a Racially Unjust America*
Kendi, Ibram X. & Reynolds, Jason	*Stamped: Racism, Antiracism, and You*
King, Martin Luther Jr	*Where Do We Go from Here: Chaos or Community?*
Lee, Harper	*To Kill A Mockingbird*
Lowery, Wesley	*They Can't Kill Us All*
Marable, Manning	*Race, Reform and Rebellion: The Second Reconstruction and Beyond in Black America 1945-2006*
Morrison, Toni	*The Origin of Others*
Noah, Trevor	*Born a Crime*
Obama, Barack	*Dreams From My Father*
Oluo, Ijeoma	*So You Want to Talk About Race*
Rothstein, Richard	*The Color of Law*
Saad, Layla F.	*Me and White Supremacy: Combat Racism, Change the World, and Become a Good Ancestor*
Tatum, Beverly Daniel	*Why Are All The Black Kids Sitting Together in the Cafeteria?*
Thomas, Angie	*The Hate You Give*
Vitale, Alex S	*The End of Policing*
Zinn, Howard	*A People's History of the United States*

Books for Teens and Children	
Author	**Title**
Celano, Marianne., Collins, Marietta & Hazzard, Ann	*Something Happened in Our Town: A Child's Story about Racial Injustice*
Cohen, Miriam	*Layla's Head Scarf (We Love First Grade!)*
Creighton, Allan & Kivel, Paul	*Helping Teens Stop Violence, Build Community, and Stand for Justice*
Edwards, Sue Bradford & Harris, Duchess	*Black Lives Matter (Special Reports)*
Ferri, Giuliano	*Brick by Brick*
Harris, Robie & Westcott, Nadine B	*Who We Are!: All About Being the Same and Being Different (Let's Talk about You and Me)*
Higginbotham, Anastasia	*Not My Idea: A Book about Whiteness (Ordinary Terrible Things*
Hoffman, Mary & Binch, Caroline	*Amazing Grace*
Gonzalez, Maya Christina	*When a Bully is President: Truth and Creativity for Oppressive Times*
Guo, Winona & Vulchi, Priya	*Tell Me Who You Are: Sharing Our Stories of Race, Culture & Identity*
Katz, Karen	*The Colors of Us*
Kissinger, Katie	*All the Colors We Are: The Story of How We Got Our Skin Color/*
Latham, Irene, Waters, Charles, Qualls, Sean	*Can I Touch Your Hair? Poems of Race, Mistakes and Friendship*
Lester, Julius & Barbour, Karen	*Let's Talk About Race*
Morrison, Toni	*Remember: The Journey to School Integration*
Nagara, Innosanto	*A is for Activist*
Perkins, Mitali	*Open Mic: Riffs on Life Between Cultures in Ten Voices*
Peters, Marilee	*Making It Right: Building Peace, Settling Conflict*
McDaniel, Breanna J., & Evans, Shane W.	*Hands Up!*
Nagara, Innosanto	*The Wedding Portrait*
Rotner, Shelley & Kelly, Sheila M	*Shades of People*
Thomas, Angie	*The Hate U Give*
Thomas, Pat & Harker, Lesley	*The Skin I'm In: A First Look at Racism*
Tyler, Michael & Lee, David	*The Skin You Live In*

Comic Books and Graphic Novels	
Author	**Title**
Barnes, Daniel & Kirkland, D.J.	*The Black Mage*
Butler, Octavia E., Duffy, Damien & Jennings, John	*Kindred: A Graphic Novel Adaptation*
Craft, Jerry	*New Kid*
Daniels Ezra Claytan & Passmore Ben	*BTTMFDRS*
Flowers, Ebony	*Hot Comb*
Johnson, Mat & Pleece, Warren	*Incognegro*
Medina, Tony, Robinson, Stacy & Jennings, John	*I Am Alfonso Jones*
Morales, Robert, Baker, Kyle & Abbott, Wes	*Truth: Red, White & Black*
Myers Walter Dean, Sims, Guy A., & Anyabwile, Dawud	*Monster: A Graphic Novel*
Osajyefo, Kwanza, Smith, Tim 3, & Igle, Jamal	*Black*
Passmore, Ben	*Your Black Friend*
Walker, David F., Brown, Chuck & Greene, Sanford	*Bitte Root*

Movies		
Title	Type	**Date**
The Great White Hope	Drama	1970
Moonlight	Drama	2016
I Am Not Your Negro	Documentary	2016
When They See Us	Biography	2019
American Son	Drama	2019
Get Out	Thriller	2017
The Namesake	Drama	2006
12 Years A Slave	Biography	2013
Malcolm X	Biography	1992
13th	Documentary	2020
Fruitvale Station	Biography	2013
Black Panther (Marvel)	Action	2018
Do the Right Thing	Drama	1989
Selma	Biography	2014
Birth of a Nation	Biography	2016
Whose Streets?	Documentary	2017
Crime + Punishment	Drama	2018
The Wire	Crime Series	2002
LA 92	Documentary	2017
Just Mercy	Biography	2019
Fences	Drama	2016
Eyes on The Prize: Then and Now	TV Movie	2016
Dark Girls	Documentary	2011
The Black List: Volume One	Documentary	2008
The Black Power Mixtape: 1967-1975	Documentary	2011
Slavery by Another Name	Documentary	2012
The Hate U Give	Drama	2018
Hidden Figures	Biography	2016
Blackklansman	Biography	2018
Mudbound	Drama	2017

Podcasts	
Title	**Hosted by**
The New York Times 1619	Nikole Hannah-Jones
Code Switch	Sidney Madden & Rodney Carmichael
Pod Save the People	DeRay
Seeing White	John Biewen
Mixed Company	Simeon Coker & Kai Deveraux Lawson
Momentum: A Race Forward Podcast	Chevon & Hiba
Higher Learning	Van Lathan and Rachel Lindsay
The United States of Anxiety	Kai Wright
74 Seconds	Minnesota Public Radio
Still Processing	Wesley Morris and Jenna Wortham
The Daily	Michael Barbaro
The Nod	Brittany Luse and Eric Eddin
The Stoop	Leila Day and Hana Baba
Identity Politics	Ikhlas Saleem & Makkah Ali
Latinos Who Lunch	FavyFav & Babelito
Long Distance	Paola Mardo
All My Relations	Matika Wilbur and Adrienne Keene
Yo, Is This Racist?	Andrew Ti
Invisibilia	Yowei Shaw & Kia Miakka Natisse
Scene on Radio	John Biewen & Chenjerai Kumanyika

Appendix G: CEO Statement

"Confronting systemic racism starts from the top." [64]

Korn Ferry CEO, Gary Burnison

> I am only one; but still I am one.
> I cannot do everything; but still can do something;
> and because I cannot do everything, I will not refuse to do the something that I can do.

I have been reflecting recently on this quotation by Edward Everett Hale, a 19th century social reformer and minister. It was sent to me several weeks ago by an executive, but it has taken on new meaning for me over the last few weeks. I've taped it to my computer screen and look at it multiple times a day. And I've been asking myself: What is the something I can do? What is the something all CEOs can do? What actions can we take?

Confronting systemic racism across America and in other parts of the world requires far more than a pledge, writing a check, or issuing a statement. That's a start, but it really takes understanding, empathy, honesty, love—and then action.

Like all of you, I am deeply saddened by the senseless killings of George Floyd, Breonna Taylor, Ahmaud Arbery, and others before them. Inexcusable and painful. My heart goes out to everyone during these times, particularly those who have personally experienced racial inequality in their own lives and in the lives of their family and friends.

We have been hosting video townhalls and webinars on race: on the first one I was joined by four black professionals from three generations from our Diversity and Inclusion business who consult with companies on driving positive change. They shared personal stories of confronting racism in their lives.

Pain, anger, rage, frustration, exhaustion…

These words were voiced repeatedly by my colleagues. I found it heartbreaking to listen to these stories of the black experience, knowing that colleagues I work with closely and their families continue to encounter racism, prejudice, fear, and injustice. I had to ask myself: What can I as a leader do about it?

Leadership is inspiring others to believe and enabling that belief to become reality. Leadership is never about you, but it starts with you—you can never improve a team or an organization unless you first improve yourself. When I think of "Leadership," I've always thought empower, not power. Except on this.

Confronting systemic racism can't be outsourced or delegated. This change must start from the top, with commitment and intentionality. Once leaders make it safe for others to speak, the ideas of how to affect change will bubble up from within. But the change and action must be driven top-down.

No one, I believe, is born to hate. Rather, I think it's quite the opposite: we're born to love. But over time, biases can form, even unconsciously. No one wants to admit this, but everyone has biases to some degree. Unless we become aware and have the courage to confront our biases, we will be at risk of staying silent and perpetuating the problem. This is a time for honesty and action. Here are some imperfect thoughts from an imperfect CEO:

1. It starts with you.

My thinking continues to evolve. Unless business leaders make this personal, change will not happen. Leaders have the voice, platform, and influence to ignite the kind of dialogue that leads to meaningful change. Systemic racism is one of the most complicated and complex problems imaginable, but it still requires an action plan—that starts with commitment and action from the top.

2. Revisit purpose.

Purpose comes next. For each of us, this goes to the quote, "The purpose of life is a life of purpose." For organizations, it is, "Why do we exist? Why are we in business?"

3. Put values into action.

Values need to guide every decision and our behavior—especially when no one is looking. The problem, however, is people are often unclear about the values—are they the same as the mission, the purpose, the culture? I can remember attending a board meeting where a senior executive was asked to explain his company's values, and he couldn't do it. Values aren't just words; they're the underpinning of an organization. Today presents a perfect opportunity to reassess how values and purpose come alive in an organization.

4. Step on the glass.

The difference between hearing and listening is comprehension. We need to be vulnerable and empathetic. Don't just react to the emotionality of the words—focus instead on understanding and owning the context and intent behind them. The fact is, when it comes to conversations about race, people feel like they're walking on glass. My view is that the glass has already been broken—so step on it and have direct conversations. If your intentions are good and you want to make a positive impact, even if you don't use the right word, trust that others will correct you—and embrace that feedback when they do. Better to say something and risk making a mistake than stay silent, which implies complicity.

5. Hear with empathy.

Action starts with empathy for each other and our experiences. "He's a six-foot-eleven basketball player, baby of the family. Every time he goes out, we worry." Mike Hyter, a black leader in our firm, told this story about his youngest son. When Ace was 13, and Trayvon Martin was killed in Florida, "that was the first time we actually had to sit down and speak to our son about the relationship between how some people will define you by your color." Since then, it's a conversation Mike and his wife have two or three times *a year* with Ace, now a rising senior who has been home since his college campus closed. Mike continued: "My wife sent an email to the neighborhood watch, basically letting people know that our son is a college student. He is at home. He's an athlete. He tends to jog and work out. She attached a picture so that people in the neighborhood would know who he was. Because she was afraid." As a parent of five children, I have my own concerns for their safety and well-being. Yet, I do not know what it's like to have *that* worry. When I listen to Mike and other colleagues, though, I can only try to imagine what it would feel like.

6. Connect.

It starts with our networks and personal lives—who are our friends? Who are the people in our circle of interaction and support?

7. Hire. Develop. Promote. Sponsor.

It's no secret what will help improve both gender equality and racial equality in the workforce, as our Women CEOs Speak research and our black P&L Leader research suggest. For leaders of color in particular, what's needed are more P&L operating roles. No one knows their true potential, however, unless they're given opportunities. We have control over who we hire, who we develop, and who we promote. To provide equality of opportunity, leaders must activate real and tangible sponsorship. Sponsors are different from mentors, who are best thought of as someone who takes others under their wings and helps them learn. Sponsors are someone higher up in the organization who can champion others to make the case for why this person should be the one who gets the assignment or promotion. In our black P&L Leader study, 86% said sponsors were essential to their professional growth, which is very similar to the results of our female leader study.

Everywhere we look, there are questions, but few answers. Yet we know that talk won't solve anything without action. This brings us back to the closing line of Hale's quotation:

I will not refuse to do the something that I can do.

What *is* the something we can do?

Appendix H: DBEI ideas for organizations

o Review your recruiting practices to ensure that it is unbiased and inclusive. For example, at the beginning of the process, remove names from resumes that are being reviewed.

o Review your performance review practices to include DBIE goals and guidelines

o Review promotion opportunities and how they are advertised and encouraged

o Review employee manuals

o Review all pay, pay increases and bonus processes

o Review how project assignments might be more equal

o Review all cultural statements and discussions;

o Review all celebrations and rituals

o Review how offices and cubicles are assigned

o Review your orientation and onboarding processes. Include and explicit section of your company approach to DBIE

o Review all marketing and promotional materials

o Review all symbols, artifacts and photos on walls

o Review all vendor cultures and processes to ensure that they are in alignment with your own

o Train managers to be aware of their own thinking and biases e.g. the difference between how someone looks and their competence/character.

o Review pay equality issues and be on the lookout for existing discrepancies

o Implement a diversity recruitment program in association with external organizations such as universities.

o Identify all stakeholders and work with everyone

o Utilize multiple approaches in parallel – and link them

o Establish a Diversity council

o Identify evangelists – of all colors

o Install a system whereby people can thank each other for a positive contribution to anti-racism.

o Educate people – about change, about the brain, about the history of racism

o Start at the top with the Board, the CEO and the Executive team.

o Educate the top tier in culture, change efforts and cultural change

o Be honest with the current reality and go public in admitting past mistakes and failures

o Honor past injustices and be the first to apologize.

- Be the first to become educated on the issue
- Be the first to change and the first to become role models.
- Publish a manifesto (or the equivalent)
- Be transparent and specific about what you are going to implement.
- Ensure that you are authentic in your approach; people see through inauthentic behavior in a heartbeat.
- Admit what you don't know and what you are going to do about it.
- Ensure that your approach is measurable and hold yourselves accountable to getting results.
- Make sure that your senior team has this as a focus and that their bonuses and pay increases are tide to the DBIE goals and guidelines
- Appoint a Chief Diversity Officer.
- Put in motion ways to become aware of what is truly going on
- Link with other similar minded local enterprises and support local community efforts
- Get coached to help understand your own biases, anchors, habits and patterns.
- Communicate, communicate, communicate – use multiple methods
- Perform a barrier and blind-spot analysis
- Publicly acknowledge the past and apologize for areas that were clearly wrong.
- Carry out a company-wide audit on the current reality
- Integrate DBIE thinking into all systems, structures, policies, procedures and processes
- Learn how to listen and ask powerful questions. That will set you up to hear what was actually being told to you rather than confirming what you wanted to hear.
- Learn how to truly collaborate – in an inclusive manner
- Find out areas of the organization have already taken positive and successful steps in the DBIE arena and leverage their work and the people involved.
- Make sure that all initiatives are broken into small, achievable parts.
- Explicitly and publicly celebrate small positive changes.
- Use each other to help identify latent biases.
- Hold conversations about ingroups within then organization and review their usefulness.
- Teach people about their brains, their comfort zones, their threats and threat responses.
- Offer your company as a guinea pig for local university and college research into DBIE

- o Appoint a Diversity committee at the Board level
- o Identify an independent third party DBIE audit group
- o Establish an independent external diversity/ethics hotline.
- o Create facilitated safe opportunities for DBIE discussions
- o Recognize that people will be changing and learning – provide education
- o And provide that education for everyone – not just leaders and managers, but all employees

References

[1] Roberts, S. O., & Rizzo, M. T. (n.d.). The Psychology of American Racism. http://doi.org/DOI: 10.1037/amp0000642

[2] Kinzler, K. D., & Spelke, E. S. (2011). Do infants show social preferences for people differing in race? *Cognition, 119*(1), 1–9. http://doi.org/10.1016/j.cognition.2010.10.019

[3] Dixon, P., & Fitzgerald, S. (2019). Understand Your Brain: For a Change. Oxford Brain Institute Press.

[4] Dixon, P., & Fitzgerald, S. (2020). Understand Your Brain: Your Brain on its Own @ Work - A Field Guide. Oxford Brain Institute Press.

[5] Rieger, T. (2020). Curing Organizational Blindness. Oxford Brain Institute Press

[6] Peebles, L. (2020). Brutality and racial bias: what the data say. *Nature, 583*, 22–24.

[7] Brookings Institute: Hamilton Project. 2016. Drug Use and Sales, by Race; Rates of Drug Related Criminal Justice Measures, by Race

[8] Brookings Institute: Hamilton Project. 2016 Op cit

[9] Desilver, D., Lipka, M., & Farmy, D. (2020, June 30). Race and policing in America: 10 things we know. Retrieved September 18, 2020, from www.pewresearch.org/fact-tank/2020/06/03/10-things-we-know-about-race-and-policing-in-the-u-s/

[10] Gramlich, J. (2020, May 6). Imprisonment rate of black Americans fell by a third from 2006 to 2018. Retrieved September 18, 2020, from pewreseacrhcenter.org

[11] Rieger, T. (2020). Op Cit

[12] Knowledge does not protect against illusory truth. Fazio, Lisa K.,Brashier, Nadia M.,Payne, B. Keith,Marsh, Elizabeth J. Journal of Experimental Psychology: General, Vol 144(5), Oct 2015, 993-1002

[13] Fazio, L. K., Rand, D. G., & Pennycook, G. (2019). Repetition increases perceived truth equally for plausible and implausible statements. *Psychonomic Bulletin & Review*, 1–19.

[14] Argyris, C. (1994). The Fifth Discipline Fieldbook: Strategies and Tools for Building a Learning Organization (1st ed.). Crown Business.

[15] https://dictionary.apa.org/ingroup-bias - downloaded on June 30, 2020

[16] Thomas Pettigrew's 1979 Paper

[17] Downloaded from UnderstandingPrejudice.org: The Psychology of Prejudice – July 1, 2020

[18] Druckman, J. N. (2001). On the Limits of Framing Effects: Who Can Frame. *The Journal of Politics, 63*(4), 1041–1066.

[19] Kathleen Nalty. Strategies for Confronting Unconscious Bias, 2016. The Colorado Lawyer, (45)

[20] Duhigg, C. (2014). The Power of Habit: Why We Do What We Do in Life and Business. Random House Trade Paperbacks.

[21] Prochaska, J. O., & DiClemente, C. C. (1983). Stages and Processes of Self-Change of Smoking: Toward an Integrative Model. *Journal of Consulting and Clinical Psychology, 51*(3), 390–395.

[22] There is an almost parallel but less detailed change model in common use that is referred to as the Competence-Incompetence/Conscious-Unconscious model. We have abandoned that. Being referred to as Unconsciously Incompetent is about as unfriendly to the brain as you can get.

[23] Cialdini, R. B. (2008). Influence: Science and Practice. Allyn and Bacon.

[24] Moore, G. (1991). Crossing the Chasm. HarperCollins.

[25] A number of people have been credited with this formula, but all of the versions appear to be derivatives of the work done by David Gleicher of Arthur D Little, in the 60's

[26] Miller, W. R., & Rollnick, S. (2013) Op Cit

[27] Miller, W. R., & Rollnick, S. (2013) Op Cit

[28] Creary, S. J. (2020). How to Be a Better Ally to Your Black Colleagues. *HBR*

[29] Roberts, S. O., & Rizzo, M. T. (2020). Op cit

[30] Roberts, S. O., & Rizzo, M. T. (2020). Op cit

[31] Humberd, B. K., Clair, J. A., & Creary, S. J. (2015). In our own backyard: when a less inclusive community challenges organizational inclusion. *Equality, Diversity and Inclusion: an International Journal, 34*(5), 395–421. http://doi.org/10.1108/EDI-11-2013-0105

[32] Comte-Sponville, A. (2002). A small treatise on the great virtues: The uses of philosophy in everyday life. Picador.

[33] Creary, S. J. (2020, September 1). How company leaders can promote racial justice in the workplace. Retrieved September 23, 2020, from https://www.strategy-business.com/article/How-company-leaders-c...o=8e2ac&utm_source=itw&utm_medium=itw20200901&utm_campaign=resp

[34] Xu, X., Zuo, X., Wang, X., & Han, S. (2009). Do You Feel My Pain? Racial Group Membership Modulates Empathic Neural Responses. *Journal of Neuroscience, 29*(26), 8525–8529. http://doi.org/10.1523/JNEUROSCI.2418-09.2009

[35] Roberts, S. O., & Rizzo, M. T. (2020). Op cit

[36] Brosnan, S. F., & de Waal, F. B. M. (2003). Monkeys reject unequal pay. Nature, 425(6955), 297–299. http://doi.org/10.1038/nature01963

[37] Andreoni, J., Aydm, D., Barton, B., Bernheim, B. D., & Naecker, J. (2016, March 22). When Fair Isn't Fair: Sophisticated Time Inconsistency in Social Preferences. Retrieved August 31, 2018, from https://docplayer.net/64596999-When-fair-isn-t-fair-sophisticated-time-inconsistency-in-social-preferences.html

[38] van den Bos, K., & Lind, E. A. (2016). The Psychology of Own Versus Others' Treatment: Self-Oriented and Other-Oriented Effects on Perceptions of Procedural Justice. Personality and Social Psychology Bulletin, 27(10), 1324–1333. http://doi.org/10.1177/01461672012710008

[39] Leigh, A., & Melwani, S. (2019). #BlackEmployeesMatter: Mega-Threats, Identity Fusion, and Enacting Positive Deviance in Organizations. *Academy of Management Review, 44*(3), 564–591. http://doi.org/10.5465/amr.2017.0127

[40] Leigh, A. E. (2020, May 5). *Am I Next? Mega-Threats, Identity Labor, and the Buffering Effect of Close Work Relationships.* (S. Melwani, Ed.). UNC Chapel Hill.

[41] Marsh, D. R., Schroeder, D. G., Dearden, K. A., Sternin, J., & Sternin, M. (2004). The power of positive deviance. *British Medical Journal, 329*, 1–3.

[42] Singhal, A., & Svenkerud, P. J. (2019). Flipping the Diffusion of Innovations Paradigm: Embracing the Positive Deviance Approach to Social Change. *Asia Pacific Media Educator, 29*(2), 151–163. http://doi.org/10.1177/1326365X19857010

[43] Leigh, A., & Melwani, S. (2019). #BlackEmployeesMatter: Mega-Threats, Identity Fusion, and Enacting Positive Deviance in Organizations. *Academy of Management Review, 44*(3), 564–591. http://doi.org/10.5465/amr.2017.0127

[44] Williams, M. T., Printz, D. M. B., & DeLapp, R. C. T. (2018). Assessing racial trauma with the Trauma Symptoms of Discrimination Scale. *Psychology of Violence, 8*(6), 1–13. http://doi.org/10.1037/vio0000212

[45] https://www.pewtrusts.org/en/research-and-analysis/blogs/stateline/2020/06/15/racism-is-a-public-health-crisis-say-cities-and-counties - accessed on July 10, 2020

[46] https://www.pewtrusts.org/ Op cit - accessed on July 10, 2020

[47] https://www.pewtrusts.org/ Op cit - accessed on July 10, 2020

[48] Spencer, S. J., Logel, C., & Davies, P. G. (2016). Stereotype Threat. *Annual Review of Psychology, 67*, 415–437.

[49] Schmader, T., Johns, M., & Forbes, C. (2008). An integrated process model of stereotype threat effects on performance. *Psychological Review, 115*(2), 336–356. http://doi.org/10.1037/0033-295X.115.2.336

[50] Dixon and Fitzgerald, 2020 Op Cit

[51] McEwen, B. S. (2016). In pursuit of resilience: stress, epigenetics, and brain plasticity. *Annals of the New York Academy of Sciences, 1373*(1), 56–64. http://doi.org/10.1111/nyas.13020

[52] Hasler, B. S., Spanlang, B., & Slater, M. (2017). Virtual race transformation reverses racial in-group bias. *Plos One, 12*(4), e0174965–20. http://doi.org/10.1371/journal.pone.0174965

[53] Shaw, A., Kenski, K., Stromer-Galley, J., Marty, R. M., Clegg, B. A., Lewis, J. E., et al. (2018). Serious Efforts at Bias Reduction. *Journal of Media Psychology, 30*, 16–28.

[54] https://www.cnn.com/2020/10/02/uk/prince-harry-meghan-racism-bhm-gbr-intl-scli/index.html

[55] Miller, W. R., & Rollnick, S. (2013). Motivational Interviewing (Third Edition). The Guildford Press.

[56] Kappes et al

[57] *Knowledge does not protect against illusory truth.* Fazio, Lisa K.,Brashier, Nadia M.,Payne, B. Keith,Marsh, Elizabeth J.
Journal of Experimental Psychology: General, Vol 144(5), Oct 2015, 993-1002

[58] Fazio, L. K., Rand, D. G., & Pennycook, G. (2019). Repetition increases perceived truth equally for plausible and implausible statements. *Psychonomic Bulletin & Review*, 1–19.

[59] https://dictionary.apa.org/ingroup-bias - downloaded on June 30, 2020

[60] Downloaded from UnderstandingPrejudice.org: The Psychology of Prejudice – July 1, 2020

[61] Druckman, J. N. (2001). On the Limits of Framing Effects: Who Can Frame. *The Journal of Politics*, 63(4), 1041–1066.

[62] Downloaded from www.wickedproblems.com on June 23, 2020.

[63] Detert, J. R. (2018). Cultivating Everyday Courage. *Harvard Business Review*, 1–10.

[64] Downloaded from https://www.kornferry.com/ceo-statement.html?utm_source=website&utm_medium=banner&utm_campaign=racism_gary on October 22, 2020

Made in the USA
Columbia, SC
23 April 2021